40
3.99

CHRISTIAN PARMA
photography

Poland

text
WOJCIECH GIEŁŻYŃSKI

◁◁ *The Podhale Region. A bewitchingly unusual sunset over Gubałówka.*

layout

BOGNA PARMA

CHRISTIAN PARMA

photography

Poland

text

WOJCIECH GIEŁŻYŃSKI

Wydawnictwo PARMA® PRESS

Zakopane. Inside the home of the Podhale glass artist, Ewelina Pęksowa.

◁ *Warsaw – Łazienki Park. The Frédéric Chopin Monument,
where Sunday concerts of Chopin's music are given in summer.*

*The Borecka Forest, a large complex ▷▷
on the edge of the Ełk Lakeland.*

Biskupin. The reconstruction of an early Slav settlement from the Hallstatt period. 25 centuries ago this settlement had about 1000 inhabitants!

Góra Ślęża. A unique archaeological monument with a pagan carving of a bear. It is from the word Ślęża that Śląsk – the Polish word for Silesia – derives.

Sobótka, a locality at the foot of Ślęża, has this stone cross of penitence.

INTRODUCTION

The Poles: History and a Touch of the Present

Poland entered Europe during a tense period. The year 1000 was soon to come. As always happens at the close of any millennium, people were scared to death of the approaching doomsday.

In King Lothar's France the great Carolingian dynasty was already nearing its end. England had its King Edgar of Wessex, too peaceful for his stormy time, since Britain was repeatedly invaded and plundered by Norman troops from Scandinavia. Having crushed the harassing bands of Magyars, Germany was growing in power under Otto I, called the Great, a sort of Chancellor Helmut Kohl of that time. Otto I was also driven by an ambition to unite not only Germany, but the whole of Europe and the whole of the Christian world. He had just then been crowned emperor.

The 10th century Poles absolutely loved it! They were just emerging out of the tribal magma and had to split with paganism as quickly as they now wish to forget communism. In order to avoid being converted to Christianity by sword, and to enter the forerunner of the European Union, they needed a protector.

Otto I was quite inclined to be such a protector. He wanted to defend himself from the savage East, constantly threatening Germany with hordes of Huns, Vandals, Avars and the like. So the Emperor gave his assent to the marriage of his vassal King of Bohemia, Boleslav the Cruel's beloved daughter Dobravka to Mieszko, some little known duke of the Polane tribe. The duke was growing in strength and it was the Polanes who began the formation of the Polish state by forcing other West Slavonic tribes to unite.

Historians are still fascinated by the question of whether the young couple had consummated their marriage before they were properly wed. Most of them favour the shameful opinion that Duchess Dobravka had shared her bed with a pagan for at least one full year before her husband was solemnly baptized. The ceremony took place most probably in Ratisbon (now Regensburg), in the year 966.

Such was Poland's way of becoming a part of Europe a thousand years ago, when the first attempt at continental integration was being made. It surely was a successful entrance, for within two years following the baptism, the Polish neophytes were sent a bishop of their own, named Jordan. Even the Bohemians, Christians already for more than a century, were granted such a privilege only five years after the Poles. It would seem quite possible that the western countries were more interested in a large Poland than in a tiny Bohemia. Maybe they saw Poland as a promising trade partner. The famous Arab traveller Ibrahim-ibn-Yaqub of Tortosa, well informed at Otto I's court, wrote that the land of Mieszko, the largest of all Slavonic dukedoms, abounded in food, especially meat and honey, and its ruler owned a strong army of three thousand warriors.

Today Poles yearn to hear journalists be similarly enthusiastic in praising the values of a country aspiring to EU membership. But in fact the West is poorly-informed. In France, Hungary is seen is a great, populous country, while Poland is a small one somewhere far to the north and east. No Frenchman would believe that "Poor, Brave Poland" is four times as large – in terms of both population and area – as Hungary, and even quite a bit bigger than Hungary, the Czech Republic, Slovakia, Lithuania, Latvia and Estonia put together.

Poland has been so unfortunate in its history that it has to strive anew for its admission to the European structures. Not all Westerners are in favour of that. As in the times of Mieszko Poland could not rid itself of the label of a postpagan country, so today, despite the popularity gained by Lech Wałęsa, it continues to be referred to as a postcommunist state.

The Poles' Coming of Age
But Poland is ever more frequently described as a "European tiger" – which sounds least convincing to the Poles themselves. Poland is far from being as wealthy as the present European Union members. Unemployment and inflation are very high, though it was not long ago that the economic growth rate was truly record-breaking. The poverty margins are shrinking. Rich and very rich people grow in number. They can easily afford a holiday on the Seychelles, skiing at Chamonix or even a mansion of their own in an imitation castle. Shops have already met Western standards. Cities and towns resemble those in Germany or France, not necessarily in tidiness, but surely in the amount of adverts for the same products as in the West. Every now and then you see a newly-built house, skyscraper or church, as well as new restaurants, bars and pubs.

In short, Poland is quickly becoming more and more like the countries it may within a few years accompany in the European Union. At the same time, many parts of Poland have maintained their traditional ways, old-fashioned charm and naturalness, to the satisfaction of Poles as well as foreign, especially Western visitors. The latter are attracted by the exotic somewhat eastern character of this country.

Poland looks Eastern to the West and Western to the East not only because it lies exactly in the geographical centre of Europe, i.e. at equal distances between Portugal and the Ural Mountains as well as from the Greek Peloponnesus and the North Cape in Norway. There are also cultural reasons: the great European borderline between the Roman and Byzantine traditions, as distinct as ever today, runs slighty west of Poland's eastern frontier. Since the dawn of history, Poland

combined its fate with that of Western civilization, at the same time constantly maintaining vivid relations with the East. From there came, for instance, old Polish trends in fashion and interior design. We can thus agree on a compromise that Poland belongs, along with the Czech Republic, Hungary and Austria, to Central Europe. This idea is extremely popular in all these countries, which had for centuries remained within the sphere of influence of the Habsburg court.

Poland is characterized by having every now and than and for shorter or longer periods, completly disappeared from the map. Its geographical contredance – the shuffle of its territory first far eastwards and then back westwards – resulted from the expansionist tendencies of its powerful neighbours. It was never easy to stand up to them, as only Poland's northern and southern borders, the sea and the mountains, are naturally strong. Other borders, unprotected by nature, were easily crossed. Therefore Polish territories were often seized by warlike peoples starting from the early Middle Ages.

The Poles' Stormy Youth
Let us go back for a short while to the beginnings of the Polish state. King Mieszko I and Dobravka had a son named Bolesław. This energetic ruler, named the Brave, managed to withstand the German pressure. At times he even kept normal and friendly relations with the Holy Roman Empire. He obtained the crown, a symbol of sovereignty, towards the end of his life in 1205. Under Bolesław the Brave ,Poland quickly grew into a big state, with more or less the same territory is has now. For a short time it also controlled Bohemia and Moravia. Gniezno and Poznań were the successive Polish capitals.

Alas, the 11th century prosperity and security of Poland turned out to be short-lived. In the following century the country was divided into several independent duchies, quite a common procedure in feudal Europe. These duchies were further subdivided. Some of them, like those of Silesia and Pomerania, drifted away from their ancient Polish roots towards Germany and Bohemia, to finally come under their rule.

In those difficult times the Mongol invasion befell Poland. At the battle of Legnica (Liegnitz) in 1241 Batu Khan's horde completely defeated the Polish knights. However, themselves decimated, the Mongols were unable to advance further west, their ultimate goal. Europe could relax and Poland's role as a bulwark of Christendom was fulfilled well for the first time. It gained this country some popularity in the West, where the Mongols were feared like fiends; they terrified the West as much as the communists did seven hundred years later.

Poland was united again in the 14th century by a modest duke of the small principality of Cujavia, Władysław the Short. He drove off various foreign rulers

Bronze statues of the Polish Piasts Mieszko I and Bolesław the Brave in the Golden Chapel of Poznań Cathedral.

Cracow and the sarcophagus of King Casimir the Great in the Wawel Cathedral.

and left a consolidated state to his son Casimir the Great, the last Polish sovereign of the Piast dynasty. Casimir put the country and its economy to order and developed trade. He is said to have found Poland built of wood and left it built of stone. He also initiated the foundation of a university in Cracow, thus linking Polish culture with the West.

But Poland lost the provinces on the River Oder to Brandenburg (later Prussia), while the Teutonic Order, spreading like a tumour over Polish, Baltic Prussian and Lithuanian land, captured the Vistula delta. Such losses could hardly be compensated for by some territorial gains in the east.

The Teutonic Knights went on expanding. They completely cut Poland off from the Baltic Sea and threatened the very existence of Lithuania. Both countries were saved by Queen Jadviga from the Hungarian branch of the Angevins. For the sake of her new homeland, she broke the engagement with her beloved Wilhelm of Habsburg and married a pagan, Grand Duke of Lithuania Władysław Jagiełło, with the result that the Lithuanians were converted to Christianity, while an alliance (and later a union) was entered into with the Poles. The united forces of both nations defeated the Teutonic Knights near Grunwald in 1410, at one of the greatest battles of the late Middle Ages. Although the Teutonic Order continued to exist for another half-century, it no longer posed a deadly threat to its neighbours and Poland entered

its Golden Age. In the 16th century it became a great power, the largest country of Europe and one of the richest.

Cracow developed into one of the most renowned cities of Europe, largely because of the excellent Cracow Academy, which still exists today. Poland became a haven for heretics, Jews and all sorts of dissidents coming from the West, for despite the domination of Roman Catholicism there were neither persecutions nor religious wars in Poland, as happened in other parts of Europe. In the mid-16th century the last Jagiellon, King Sigismund Augustus, voiced a statement to his subjects that none of his contemporary monarchs would dare to pronounce: "I am not the king of your conscience".

Following the end of the Jagiellonian dynasty, a system of electing kings by the nobility was introduced. The vast numbers of Polish noblemen, endowed with many rights and privileges, preferred to choose foreign kings from famous European families. This fostered the development of foreign relations, but was certainly bad for the administration of the state. Poland's system at that early time already resembled later republican states, in which monarchs were replaced by presidents with limited powers. The role of the Sejm, the Polish parliament of the nobility, grew steadily. Its state-killing rule of liberum veto allowed any individual deputy to cease the debate and paralyse the governing process.

The Golden Age in Poland was marked by the foundation of the Cracow Academy. The Collegium Minus of the present Jagiellonian University.

Fortified Jasna Góra Monastery, which resisted the Swedish invasion in the 17th century.

The 17th century was therefore far less prosperous for Poland, a country with weak governance and a growing number of conflicts. To the east the Grand Duchy of Muscovy, the precursor of Russia, was expanding rapidly. The Ukraine, then under Polish rule, underwent a great Cossack rebellion. The Swedish invaded Poland from the north and for several years occupied the whole country along with its new capital, Warsaw. They could only not seize the Jasna Góra fortified monastery at Częstochowa, the sanctuary of the Holy Virgin Mary. This made Her the main object of a cult in the Polish Roman Catholic rite. To this day, millions of Poles go on pilgrimages to Jasna Góra, which is known as "the Polish Lourdes".

In addition, Poland was raided by the Turkish and Tartar armies – now winning, now being defeated. The last great triumph over the Turks was achieved by the famous Polish heavy cavalry – the hussars – led by King John III Sobieski in the crucial battle of Vienna in 1683. By saving Vienna, Poland acted as a liberator of Europe and a bulwark of Christianity for the second time.

The Fall and Revival of the Poles
The 18th century was disastrous for Poland. Under the weak rule of the Saxon dynasty the central authority dwindled and internal affairs were in a complete mess. The "noble democracy" turned into anarchy and each aristocratic family carried out its own egocentric policy. The Russian, Swedish and Prussian armies roamed freely

over Polish land. It was not until the end of the century that the Poles seemed to wake up and made some attempts to reform education, the army and the economy. The crowning achievement was the 3rd May Constitution of 1791, being very progressive for that time. The world's second – after the American – and Europe's first constitutional act, it was aimed at steering the country out of chaos and modernizing its system.

But the national spurt came too late. After three partitions – in 1772, 1792 and 1795 – Poland, torn apart by Russia, Prussia and Austria, disappeared from the map. Some hope emerged during the time of Napoleon Bonaparte. The Poles formed an army of more than a hundred thousand soldiers and fought at his side till the battle of Leipzig, known as the Battle of Nations. Three quarters of the Polish soldiers were killed or taken prisoner. The fate of Poland was sealed at the Congress of Vienna in 1815. No such country was to exist for a hundred years to follow.

Very soon the Poles rose to fight for their independence. The first rising took place in response to the Second Partition of 1792. It was led by Tadeusz Kościuszko, a hero of two nations, as he had earlier fought for the independence of the United States. The next and greatest Polish armed uprising in November 1830 saved... Belgium, for it stopped the tsarist army from proceeding to suppress the rebellion in that country. When the Russians seized Warsaw in 1831, the French minister Sebastiani made his famous, or rather infamous statement: "L'ordre regne a Varsovie".

Not always was the West so cynical about Poland, however. Thousands of Polish refugees found their refuge on the banks of the Seine, Thames, Moselle, Rhine and Tiber. When another insurrection broke out in January 1863, a few hundred Western volunteers joined the Polish units.

But this rising also ended in failure. Numerous Poles were hanged, thousands of them were sent into exile to Siberia. Thus, the future Great War of Nations, a dream envisaged by the national bard Adam Mickiewicz, remained the only solution.

From the Poles' point of view, the 1914-18 war ended in a miracle. All three partitioning powers were defeated and disintegrated. The dreams of generations came true: the Polish state was revived. Its first head of state was Józef Piłsudski. He had started his fight for independence in the underground Polish Socialist Party. During the First World War he commanded the Legions formed within the Austro-Hungarian army. However, after driving the Russians out of central Poland, Piłsudski let the Legions he had formed so laboriously dissolve, for he intended to shift his political ground. Towards the end of the war he took the side of the Western Allies, already supported by other Polish military formations in France.

The attitude of the United States President Woodrow Wilson played an important role in the rebirth of Poland. In his presidential address of January 1917 he declared that Poland should be united and independent. This became a reality on 11 November 1918.

However, Poland was soon bound to face another dramatic trial: the Bolshevik invasion in 1920. In the battle of Warsaw, the young Polish Army managed to repel the units of General Tukhachevsky, who had been planning to conquer Germany and the rest of Europe. He did not even cross the Vistula. For the third time in history Poland acted as a bulwark.

After a century and a half of slavery, Poland was coming back to life with difficulty, but the Poles enjoyed their "regained mess", as it was described by the writer Juliusz Kaden-Bandrowski. The first years of integration and reconstruction of the country were auspicious. The Poles are known for their powers of improvisation. Unfortunately, persistence is not their main virtue. Poland was plagued by political disputes, government crises, workers' protests and peasant riots. In 1926 Marshal Piłsudski staged a military coup, which earned him a very unfavourable opinion in the West. This opinion, still adhered to sometimes, is not quite fair. His authoritarian rule never resembled fascism, which already controlled Italy and was soon to infect Germany, Portugal, Spain and other countries. Although personally Piłsudski hated "Sejmocracy", the parliamentary system was maintained

in Poland. It is quite possible that his coup saved the country from totalitarianism, towards which the extreme right wing had been heading.

Down again

Twenty years of independence healed Poland. The integration of the former partition zones was unexpectedly quick. Modern industrial works and the large port of Gdynia were built. Poland formed a strong army and was the first state to resist Hitler's aggression. His attack on Poland on 1. September 1939 unleashed the Second World War. Invaded by Stalin from the other side, Poland was soon overwhelmed, but its soldiers would never stop fighting. Some Polish divisions took part in the defence of France. Polish soldiers fought at Narvik in Norway and defended Tobruk in Libya. They achieved great success in the Italian campaign by capturing the major German bastion at Monte Cassino. Polish aircraft pilots fought magnificently in the Battle of Britain. On many seas sailors fought under the white and red flag. Polish armoured units took part in the liberation of France, Belgium and Holland. Polish divisions set up within the Red Army finally came as far as Berlin. In occupied Poland the struggle was carried on by underground forces and forest partisans of the Home Army, formed by the London government in exile. Two insurrections broke out in the capital: the rising in the Jewish Ghetto in 1943 and the Warsaw Uprising in 1944. Both were put down by the Germans. The Soviet army, watching the bloodbath in 1944 from the other bank of the Vistula, did not come forward with help. It was Stalin's plan to let the Poles bleed to death in their unequal struggle with the Germans. Only the Western Allies tried to airdrop some weapons and ammunition to the Warsaw insurgents.

The uprising ended in the slaughter of a few hundred thousand inhabitants of Warsaw and the city's total destruction. Altogether, the Second World War claimed about six million casualties in Poland, half of them people of Jewish origin murdered by the Nazis in the ghettos and above all in the concentration camps. Of these camps, Auschwitz will forever remain the symbol of the Holocaust.

Although a member of the victorious coalition, Poland turned out to be one of its most tragic victims. The country's fate was decided upon by the superpowers at the conferences in Yalta and Potsdam. Washington and London pretended to believe in Uncle Joseph's good intentions (it is hardly probable that they really did) and they actually left Poland under his control. Poland lost more eastern territories to the Soviet Union than it gained as compensation from Germany in the west. Anyway, the land given to the USSR was populated mostly by Ukrainians and Byelorussians. Poland's real disaster was the loss of independence and the imposing of the communist system on the country for the next 45 years. Poland, now totally dependent on Moscow, stayed economically backward even as compared with such countries as Spain, Greece and Portugal, much poorer than it was in the period between the world wars.

Unlike in other countries of the socialist bloc, the Soviet Union never managed to bring the communist system in Poland close to any perfection, facing the strong resistance of the Polish society. In spite of repression, the Catholic church survived and even grew stronger, becoming a spiritual bastion of the persecuted nation. Individual farming was also saved. Polish culture has been enriched by many excellent artists and authors. The communists were never really able to cut off Polish contacts with the West. Among other reasons, millions of Polish immigrants living in those countries would always support the aspirations of their compatriots in Poland.

Just as in the 19th century partition period, Poles frequently rose up in rebellion, but armed rising was replaced with worker strikes and demonstrations as well as clandestine conspiracy by the intelligentsia. The first wave of protests in 1956 forced the communists to abandon the Stalinist methods of terror. Student riots in 1968 and worker protests in 1970 helped overthrow the autocratic party leader Władysław Gomułka. They also stimulated a superficial opening of the country to Western ways and consumerism by his successor Edward Gierek. After the mass demonstrations of workers in 1976, dissident organizations of the opposition started to act quite openly. More and more underground books and press were published.

Once Again Reborn

It all exploded in August 1980 in the form of the Solidarity movement (started in Gdańsk under the leadership of Lech Wałęsa), which was soon to reach 10 million members. To the amazement and admiration, but also a certain degree of concern of the West, Solidarity questioned the whole post-Yalta order with ever growing courage. This political enthusiasm was closely connected with the election of the Polish Pope, Karol Wojtyła, who visited his homeland as Pope John Paul II a year before the "Polish August" of 1980 and thereby encouraged the nation. Gathering by the millions at their native Pope's side, Poles could feel their own power.

That was the beginning of the end of communism in Poland. And worldwide, too, for by a lucky coincidence the new U.S. President Ronald Reagan's personal goal happened to be the dismantling of the Soviet Empire. Though the Soviet system had already disintegrated from within, its fall was accelerated by two events: one, and the most important, was the increase of American armaments, which the USSR could not keep pace with. The other was the birth of the Solidarity union, which provided inspiration for other enslaved countries. Even the introduction of martial law in Poland by General

Brzezinka (Birkenau) held a sub-camp of the parent Oświęcim (Auschwitz) Concentration Camp. This is a characteristic railway loading platform.

Monument to the Jewish Ghetto Uprising in Warsaw.

Warsaw. The Monument to the Fallen and Murdered in the East.

The birth of Solidarity initiated the new Springtime of Nations in Europe.

Lech Wałęsa, the leader of fighting Solidarity, later the President of free Poland.

Wojciech Jaruzelski could not stop the clock of history running. Though weakened by countless arrests of its leaders, Solidarity continued to work underground. At that time the underground press became a Polish speciality and the number of book and newspaper titles in illegal, or "second" circulation amounted to thousands. In 1989 Poland initiated the new Springtime of Nations in Europe. Pressed by society, the communists agreed to the "round table" talks with the opposition and to partly free elections. The elections, unprecedented behind the Iron Curtain, ended in the utter failure of the communists. The Polish United Workers' Party, which used to control the government in Poland, was self-dissolved. Still formally a member of the Warsaw Pact, Poland established its first non-communist government headed by Tadeusz Mazowiecki. The government carried out a shock free-market reform. A year later Lech Wałęsa, an ordinary electrician, was elected president.

Poland was followed by others. The Berlin wall crumbled. The "peace and socialism bloc" ceased to exist. The USSR collapsed.

Francis Fukuyama announced the end of history.

A bit too early, though. The liberal reforms were successful, but they caused a considerable increase in unemployment, unknown to the East-European societies before. Inflation rose and living standards fell for a time. In some countries, including Poland, postcommunists disguised as social democrats or liberals came back to power by means of democratic elections. The pendulum of public opinion swings to the right, and then to the left. In 1999 Poland joined NATO, and on 1 May 2004 it became a member of the European Union.

Let Some Old Ways Remain

Polish mountains are not as high and majestic as the Alps, but the Tatras, although much lower, match the Alps in the menacing beauty of their rocky crags. The Polish sea is not warm, like the Mediterranean, but its fine beaches are of rare beauty. Siberia certainly has more primeval forests, but the Białowieża Forest (stretching into Belarussian territory) is the wildest of all. Indeed, where else can you meet a huge hairy bison face to face?

Tourists visiting Poland value its naturalness most of all. It is true that two thirds of Poles now live in cities and the country is losing its fabled idyllic atmosphere, but civilization at its fullest has not yet – fortunately – infected many corners of Poland. To be honest, local inhabitants of such places are less happy about it than visitors from the West.

"Oh, a horse!" my French acquaintance gave such a shout of joy every time he saw that animal pulling a plough – a view still quite common in the Polish countryside, though far less common now than a tractor. "Oh, a hare!" he almost fainted when he saw a grey hare hopping about at leisure next to my country house in the Masurian Lakes. And when he saw a huge plate filled with crayfish freshly pulled out of the River Krutynia, he became nervous, for he calculated that in Paris such a feat would cost him two days' work. And here it was free, fresh from the water.

Hunters – not my favourites – are as excited about coming to Poland as about going on an African safari. Still, they are not bound to see a bear (unless high in the mountains if they are extremely lucky), although many people in the West believe Poland is nothing but snow and bears.

Karol Wojtyła (1920-2005), the Polish Pope John Paul II gives spiritual support to the Roman Catholic majority of Polish society.

A paradise for ornithologists and bird-watchers it certainly is! Any small village surrounded by marshy meadows can have as many stork nests as the whole of Denmark. They are a distinguishing mark of the Polish countryside. A very rare species of black stork can also be encountered, as well as cormorants, herons and cranes. There are still some wild eagles, though today they are more often seen on the Polish national emblem. The Vistula is an attraction as one of the last unregulated large rivers of Europe. If only its waters were clearer...

Ethnographers and admirers of folklore will find in Poland such rarities as wooden churches and cottages, colourful church festivals and beautiful folk costumes, which have survived only in some regions. It is much worse with the folk song tradition, as the young generation now goes in for disco, techno and rock.

One tradition, said to be a national feature of the Poles, is available for every visitor: Polish hospitality. They are particularly generous in the regions where foreign visitors are not very common, thus being a great attraction for the locals. On the other hand, many border towns in Poland are very hospitable to crowds of visitors from abroad – Ukraine, Russia, Lithuania, Belarus, the Czech Republic and even Germany – who only come for a day to do their shopping. For them it is cheaper in Poland and everything is in good supply. You can even buy the world's biggest plaster-of-Paris dwarfs – popular garden ornaments in Germany.

Hotels are no longer cheap. Their prices – though not always those of the services – are now comparable with those in the West. In summer, the most frequented tourist localities offer quite inexpensive rooms and whole houses to let. Bungalows and tents at camping sites or bivouacs are still cheaper. Let us set out on a journey then. For the time being it will be a journey through all the regions of Poland, from the sea to the mountains, as shown in the pictures of this book.

The Suwałki Region with its characteristic erratics (giant boulders ▷▷ dropped by melting glaciers at the end of the Ice Age).

THE GOLDEN BEACHES COAST

Trzęsacz, where we visit the famous clifftop ruins of a 14th century church "claimed by the sea".

Rewal. Fishing boats.

Stargard Szczeciński is a Western Pomeranian town with a mediaeval architectural plan. The two-towered Church of the Blessed Virgin Mary dates back to the Gothic period.

Not many Poles are aware of having their own mini-archipelago: several small islands where the border River Oder flows into the Baltic. They are neither so beautiful nor so extensive as the Canary or Balearic Islands, but the two largest of them – Uznam and Wolin – have some very fashionable beaches at Świnoujście and Międzyzdroje, almost on the border with Germany. A greater part of Uznam belongs to that country, while Poland owns but a tiny eastern area of the island. As long as Poland bordered the German Democratic Republic, the two neighbours kept arguing about a narrow channel in the Baltic leading to Świnoujście port. The argument was accompanied by hostile demonstrations of the "fraternal" navies. The problem has totally disappeared now that Poland has Federal Germany as its neighbour. Polish relations with the Germans are more friendly than they have ever been since 1000, the year Emperor Otto III paid a visit to Bolesław the Brave at Gniezno. The duke (not yet king) acquired independence from the German church hierarchy and was granted the status of the Emperor's close partner in ruling over the Holy Roman Empire.

The beaches are popular among the Germans and still more among the Swedes, who come here by ferry from Ystad. The south coast of the Baltic seems much warmer to the Swedes than to the Poles.

Wolin's attraction is the national park, a habitat of many species of bird, including birds of prey such as the sea eagle. In the 10th century the small fishermen's settlement of Wolin served as an important trading port. According to contemporary chroniclers, it had 12 gates and could allow 300 ships at a time into the harbour. The ships sailed to England, Byzantium and Novgorod. Some Persian coins, Egyptian beads and remains of an old lead glass smelting shop – a great technological achievement for those times – have been excavated in the area by archaeologists. A lighthouse called Vulcan's Pot rose above the port. It lit the way for the Pomeranian tribe of the Wolinianie (Velunzani). After some bitter struggles, they joined the Polish state under the Piasts for a short time. But they mostly formed an alliance with the Slavic federation of the Veleti, spreading westwards nearly as far away as Denmark.

Świnoujście is not only a seaside resort, but primarily an outer port of the major city of Szczecin, situated 60 kilometres to the south on the River Oder. Szczecin's connections with Poland were not long-lasting either. The town had its own, pagan dukes. The 10th century chronicler Herbord described the local temple of their Three-headed god. When Wolin declined in the 11th century, Szczecin grew into a sizeable and rich port town. It became the seat of the most powerful of all Pomeranian dukedoms. Threatened by German expansionism, this small state maintained friendly relations with Poland. During the period of feudal disintegration it surrendered to the Brandenburgs and Danes. Later it was conquered by the Swedes and Prussians, and even the French during the Napoleonic Wars. And also by the Red Army, which seized Szczecin in the last days of the Second World War to pass it to Poland very reluctantly some time later, plundered and devastated.

Szczecin is distinguished by its urban design modelled in accordance with the solutions of the famous town planner Haussmann during the 19th century rebuilding of Paris. It is characterized by star-shaped squares with radiating wide avenues lined with trees.

The city, situated on the left bank of the Oder in the north-westernmost corner of Poland, is like a gate to the North European countries. Owing to the rapid development of trade with Germany and the inflow of tourists in recent years, Szczecin has expanded and grown rich. It has become an arena of international life.

Opposite Wolin Island on the right bank of the River Dziwna, which in fact is a strait, lies the little old town of Kamień Pomorski. In the past it was also the seat of a duke and a bishop. In the Romanesque-Gothic cathedral internationally renowned festivals of organ and chamber music are held. East of Kamień Pomorski, 400 kilometres of wonderful beaches stretch along the seashore. The sea is not azure but usually grey, nevertheless to many artists, especially marine painters, it looks exceptionally beautiful. They prefer the soft palette of sand dunes overgrown with pine trees bent and twisted by the wind to the bright colours of the Riviera or the lifeless symmetry of Levant cypresses. This landscape is more like graphic art than painting. Even the clear sky has less glow than in the Mediterranean, and when it becomes cloudy, you can really feel the severity of the northern seas. If you prefer Bruegel to Gaugin, you are bound to fall in love with the Baltic.

A line of fishing villages and tourist resorts string along the never-ending strand of beaches. Each place has its devotees: Dziwnów, Pobierowo, Rewal, Niechorze, Mrzeżyno and Trzęsacz on a high cliff washed away by sea waves, so that the old Gothic church once a mile away from the sea has now almost completely collapsed into the Baltic. The nearby town of Kołobrzeg is a popular health resort, frequented by Swedish tourists. The town, dating from the 8th century, was the seat of one of the first Polish bishoprics from 1000. During the Second World War, after fierce fighting, Kołobrzeg was captured by the troops of the 1st Polish Army coming together with the Red Army. The town was nearly totally destroyed. Fortunately, after the war it was reconstructed and made a real town of gardens by its young and enthusiastic architects.

More summer resorts are found further to the east: Ustronie Morskie, Sarbinowo and Mielno, Unieście on the sandbar between the sea and Lake Jamno, the fishing port of Darłowo, Jarosławiec, and the most favoured: Ustka and Łeba. The two towns are engaged in a seething dispute about which of them deserves the title of the summer capital of Poland. As a matter of fact, both do.

The Słowiński National Park begins on the outskirts of Łeba. The main attraction in the park are mobile high dunes, the highest of which, at Czołpin, rises up to 56 metres. They form a true desert in miniature. The sand travels with the wind, fighting a victorious battle against the plant life. Wide expanses of forest have already fallen victim to it. The nearby large Lake Łebsko with its shores dense with vegetation and famous for its multitude of water birds, is excellent for sailing. Some more coastal lakes, divided from the sea by narrow strips of land, lie in the neighbourhood. The village of Kluki, formerly owned by one large family, the Kluks, has a skansen museum of the Slovincian people, a small Pomeranian tribe which managed to resist Germanization and keep their own language till the early 20th century. Some fisher families claim to have Slovincian ancestry, even though they cannot speak their language any more, and have learnt to speak Polish.

A line of smaller and bigger coastal towns has developed from medieval settlements built at a safe distance from the sea. The very sea shore, plundered by the Scandinavian pirates called Vikings, was too dangerous to settle. The history of such towns as Gryfice, Białogard, Koszalin, Sławno and Lębork dates back to the Middle Ages. Fragments of sacral buildings and fortifications from that time have been preserved. Słupsk, apart from its historic monuments, has also made a name for its excellent "Słupsk inns", in which the tradition of Slovincian and Kashubian cuisine is carried on. Similar inns with fine stylized interiors have been opened in other Polish towns and some of their ornamental elements are even sold abroad.

The region to the south, called the Pomeranian Lake District – unlike the Mazurian Lake District – has not yet been discovered by tourists. It was not until a few years ago that large areas of this region, including forests, lakes and towns, became accessible to Poles. Some old towns were not even shown on any map. These were the territories of Soviet troops stationing in Poland – their bases and military training grounds. When the Warsaw Pact was dissolved and the Red Army left for Russia in 1992, the Poles were astonished to learn that they had a new town: Borne-Sulinowo. Until then a secret locality, it was left deserted. A lot of people, especially the young and homeless, came to settle here, but in order to live they also needed jobs. Year by year, the Polish Far West has slowly been adapting to a normal life. Country houses and camping sites have appeared on newly acquired lakes; you can pick blackberries in former "no access" forests. You must be very cautious, though, not to step on a land mine or a grenade.

The Drawsko Lake District is unusually picturesque. Its beautifully situated health resort, Połczyn Zdrój is known for its mild climate and curative mineral water. The Bytów Lake District is almost equally charming. The largest lake of the region is Miedwie near Szczecin. Its bottom is as deep as 28 metres below sea level.

Kamień Pomorski is a health resort on the Kamień Lagoon. Here we see the imposing Baroque organ in the city's stone and brick Gothic-style Cathedral.

The Baltic. The picturesque seashore at Dziwnów ▷ may leave the visitor spellbound.

Kołbacz. The Gothic Cistercian Abbey complex
from the 13th-15th centuries.

Szczecin is a large commercial port and centre
of shipbuilding on the Szczecin Lagoon. Its Old Market
Square boasts a 15th century Town Hall.

Szczecin. The Gothic portal to the Cathedral
of St. James the Apostle, rebuilt in the years
1971-1975 following wartime destruction.

Szczecin. The Renaissance castle of the Dukes ▷
of Pomerania is multi-winged, with two courtyards. It was rebuilt post-1945.

Międzyzdroje is a fashionable place of seaside recreation.

Dziwnówek. Polish Windsurfing Championships.

Sarbinowo. During a sweltering summer, the warm sea simply invites one in to bathe.

◁ *Pogorzelica, a sea-bathing and recreativnal resort.*

Darłowo is an old fishing port. The 14th century Gothic Castle of the Dukes of Pomerania here boasts a 24-metre gate tower.

Mielno is on the Słowiński Coast, a popular sea bathing area. ▷ Słowiński National Park by the Baltic coast has been recognised as ▷▷ a Biosphere Reserve by UNESCO. Its mobile dune fields are a major attraction.

*Stargard Szczeciński and the Gothic interior
of its St. Mary's Church from the 13th century.*

*Nowogard is a town on Lake Nowogardzkie whose history ▷
stretches back to the 10th century.*

Drawsko Pomorskie. Bestiaries baked in brick in the side portal of the 14th century church.

THE LAND OF AMBER AND COPERNICUS

The Vistula widens into the Włocławek Reservoir in front of a great dam, which was meant to start the "cascadization" of the river. Several other dams with sluice-gates and water turbines were planned. Due to a lack of funds, the first dam was the only one constructed. Some claim this is just good for the Vistula, which has remained the wildest river in Europe, to the advantage of tourists, anglers and ornithologists, as well as all aesthetes and traditionalists.

In no circumstances should you miss Ciechocinek, the most famous saline spa in Poland. In the early 19th century three graduation towers for brine were constructed here: huge wooden frames packed with branches. Brine flows down the branches and salt is deposited. The area around, saturated with salt and iodine molecules and when it is sunny also healthy ozone, forms a kind of gigantic inhalation site. Apart from their medicinal properties, the towers are a unique example of such construction in the world.

Going down the Vistula we arrive in Toruń, a town closely associated with Nicolaus Copernicus. Suddenly we are in the Middle Ages. The entire old centre of Toruń is a historic monument of international rank and there is no other Gothic town like this in Poland.

The well-preserved town hall was built in the 13th/14th centuries and rebuilt at the beginning of the 17th century in the Mannerist style by the famous Dutch architect A. van Obbergen. Close by at 17 Kopernika (Copernicus) Street the greatest astronomer of all time was born in 1473. Although he wrote in German or Latin, he always considered himself a Pole. He was also a physician, administrator, mathematician, economist and canon. The church, however, objected strongly to his heliocentric concept of the universe and pronounced it dangerous for the religious outlook, although it was accepted by such scholars as Giordano Bruno, Galileo and Kepler. His work De revolutionibus... was not removed from the index of forbidden books until 1828. From that year on the Earth could continue going round the Sun without committing a sin.

Other treasures of Gothic architecture include the 13th century St. John's Church with its beautiful authentic wall paintings, the early-14th century monumental Basilica of St. James, and the oldest of them – the Church of the Virgin Mary. Fragments of defensive walls as well as numerous gates, bastions and towers have been preserved in Toruń.

Ciechocinek, a famous spa since the 19th century. A flower clock in the Spa Park.

Toruń. The Monument to Copernicus stands before the Gothic Town Hall on the Old Town Market Square.

Malbork. This relief decoration of the Golden Gate portal to the High Castle presents the Wise and Foolish Virgins.

Only 50 kilometres away from Toruń lies the rival town of Bydgoszcz, the biggest river port in Poland. Here, via a canal, the Vistula system is connected with the inland water routes of Western Europe. River navigation plays a marginal role in the Polish transport system, though. Bydgoszcz is larger than Toruń and its beginnings go back to the 13th century. The town's historic places include the late-Renaissance Church of the Poor Clares and a complex of 18th century granaries.

On the Nogat, a branch of the Vistula, towers the huge castle-monastery of Malbork, the main stronghold and capital of the Teutonic state. A great attraction for tourists, it was about the greatest fortress built in medieval Europe.

The Żuławy region in the delta of the Vistula between the river branches has the best alluvial soil in Poland, deposited by the Vistula. The region, lying below sea level, was often flooded in the past, when people did not know how to build strong embankments. Elbląg, a town at the eastern edge of the Żuławy, had unsuccessfully competed with Gdańsk in the Baltic trade before it lost its importance as a port.

Gdańsk is one of three cities in Poland, next to Warsaw and Cracow, which have a worldwide reputation. There are two reasons for this. The first reason is that here in Gdańsk the first shots in the Second World War were fired by the German training battleship Schleswig-Holstein at 4.45 am on 1st September 1939. The shots were directed at the Polish military post and depot on the Westerplatte Peninsula – a Polish enclave within the territory of the Free City of Danzig under the provisions of the Treaty of Versailles. The city was officially supervised by the League of Nations but had in fact come under the control of the Nazis. The Polish outpost, manned by 182 soldiers, resisted the attacks from land, sea and air by German forces twenty times stronger for a whole week. The Battle of Westerplatte is now given in history textbooks as an example of Polish soldiers' greatest deeds.

Another reason for Gdańsk's popularity was the far-famed strike in the Gdańsk Shipyard led by Lech Wałęsa. It started on 14 August 1980 and resulted in the first ever agreement concluded between the government and the protesting workers in the history of communist countries, as well as the formation of the Solidarity union. More strikes in 1988 resulted in the "round table" talks of the communists with their political adversaries. The talks fostered the triumph of democracy in Poland and other countries of Eastern Europe. In those years Gdańsk was the main bastion of Polish opposition, and it is still the headquarters of the Independent, self-administered Trade Union called Solidarity.

Naturally, the history of Gdańsk and its region began much earlier – two thousand years ago in fact. The Polish nation did not then exist. The land, populated by numerous proto-Slavic and Baltic tribes, was visited by caravans of merchants from as far away as ancient Rome. According to Pliny, the first of them was sent by the cruel emperor Nero himself, who got so enchanted by a light yellowish stone he saw on a slave woman's alluring bosom, that he arranged a great expedition to the "northern barbarians". Bold merchants crossed the Alps, then the Danube at Vindobona (today Vienna), and arrived at the settlement of Calisia (today the town of Kalisz), where they bought some amber. As it was too little for the imperial court's needs, they proceeded further, crossed the Vistula (which in English has retained the Latin name) and reached the present Gdańsk area, or maybe as far as the Sambia Peninsula, which isn't in Poland.

A small village could have existed at the present site of Gdańsk as early as the 9th or even 8th century. However, at that time a mysterious port of Truso, described by traveller Wulfstan, dominated in the region and grew into a mighty settlement in the 10th century, only to disappear without trace. It might have lain somewhere on a deep gulf which later formed Lake Drużno, reportedly the richest in birds of all lakes in Europe.

At about that time, in The Life of St. Adalbert, dated 997, a name of unknown origin and difficult to pronounce appeared: Gyddanyzc. Modified into Kdanzc and then Gdantz, it finally became Danzig in German and Gdańsk in Polish.

It was already a big and cosmopolitan city, inhabited by Pomeranians and Poles, then also by some Germans and numerous Flemish, Scottish and other settlers from the West. Gdańsk was a member of the Hanseatic League, which exercised a great commercial and military power over the North Sea and the Baltic. During the Polish-Teutonic wars the dwellers of Gdańsk, though to a great degree Germanized, were on the side of Poland and drove the Teutonic Knights away. It turned out to be a profitable move, for Poland was becoming a leading exporter of farm produce and forest crops in Europe. Goods were floated along the Vistula to Gdańsk. The town grew rich and expanded in the fine Flemish style. It became a major centre of culture, science and printing. Gdańsk astronomer Johan Hevelius, honoured with awards by Louis XIV of France, Charles II of England and the Pope, was famed all over Europe. Gabriel Fahrenheit, the inventor of a thermometer, also started his career in Gdańsk. After the first partition of Poland in 1772, Gdańsk remained part of Poland – an enclave separated from it by the Prussian partition zone (almost like a free city).

Most of Gdańsk's inhabitants were Protestants and spoke German, but they felt offended if someone called them Prussians. They regarded themselves simply as Gdańsk people – the city was their homeland.

Gdańsk was given the status of a free city for the first time under Napoleon Bonaparte, who visited it in 1807 after the seizure of the town from Prussian hands and was greeted enthusiastically. A similar status, though not granted officially, had been enjoyed by Gdańsk under Polish kings. After the fall of Napoleon, Gdańsk went back to Prussia and became an ordinary, provincial town. It became a free city again between the First and the Second World Wars. Regained by Poland in 1945, it was all in ruins. In a few years it was rebuilt with great care and attention to its historic architecture, mostly Gothic and the Flemish Mannerism. The Gdańsk Old Town is a beautiful place for sightseeing, especially the Long Market route from the Golden Gate to the Green Gate

(a remainder of the defensive walls standing in the old port on the Motława), with unique restored medieval granaries. The main sacred building is the monumental Gothic Church of the Holy Virgin Mary.

The former health resort of Sopot, with a casino almost as famous as that in Monte Carlo, today serves as a summer mecca for all Poles, especially during the International Song Festival held every summer at the Forest Opera.

The third city, Gdynia, is completely different. It was built in the early 1920s along with the port, which at the end of the following decade was already the busiest harbour in the Baltic Sea.

When the weather is fine, the view from the hills around the Tri-city extends as far as the Hel Peninsula, a 30-kilometre-long narrow stretch of land resembling a scythe, which, like many villages south of the Tri-city, is inhabited by the Kashubians, the remainder of the old Pomeranian tribe, who resisted a thousand years of Germanization and Polonization to preserve their own dialect, hardly understandable to Poles.

Another narrow sandbar with many bathing beaches in the vicinity of Gdańsk lies at the Vistula mouth, separating the Baltic Sea from the Vistula Lagoon.

Gdynia Orłowo with its elevated cliff coastline so unsual for Poland.

◁ Pelplin was once the seat of Poland's Cistercian order. The 1837 Bishop's Palace stands in extensive parkland by the River Wierzyca.

Pelplin's most precious piece of heritage is the imposing Cathedral from the 13th and 14th centuries, as well as the associated monastery buildings and Gothic-style cloisters.

Toruń, once part of the Hanseatic League, is an old town with a wealth of heritage buildings. Here Podmurna Street in the Mediaeval quarter of the city.

Bydgoszcz on the Brda, a 15th and 16th century centre ▷▷ of the grain and salt trade. Urban architecture on the river bank.

The Elbląg Canal in the area of the Buczyniec Incline.

Malbork. The interior of the western
Gallery of the High Castle.

Malbork, a town set up by the Teutonic Knights on the Nogat. The castle built ▷
in the 13th-15th century, one of the most outstanding examples of medieval fortification architecture.

*Golub-Dobrzyń boasts a 14th century castle remodelled in Renaissance style in the 1600s.
Each year, this plays host totournaments of jousting and other chivalrous skills.*

*Kwidzyn has a monumental Gothic castle of brick, together with
a fortified cathedral built by the Order of the Teutonic Knights.*

*The Chełm Lakeland is characterised by a large number of small ▷
lakes, as well as extensive marshlands.*

Jastarnia is a recreational and spa resort on the Hel Peninsula.

Chałupy. Gulls on a breakwater.

Hel. Grey seal: a species of coastal areas of the North-East Baltic Sea and North Atlantic.

Gdańsk. The Neptune Fountain on Długi Targ (the Long Market). ▷
Gdańsk, a historic port with magnificent old architecture. Długi Targ Street, teeming with life despite the late hour. ▷▷

FINLAND IN MINIATURE

The Suwałki region is a picturesque land with deep lakes.

Grunwald. Latter-day knights meet on the battlefield every year in order to recreate the famous victory.

Wigry. The Baroque-style post-Cameldolite monastery complex by Lake Wigry.

Other countries have higher mountains, warmer seas and more ancient historic relics than Poland. But such an amassment of lakes as in Mazury is hardly met in any other country except Finland and Sweden.

The lakes are of various types. The largest, Lake Śniardwy (109 km²) looks like a little sea with dangerous crested waves. There are a lot of smaller lakes of the same type, with countless bays, promontories and islets. There are still more long and narrow ribbon lakes and numerous tiny pools entirely hidden in woods, dense shrubs or reeds.

Connected by small rivers and canals, they form a vast system of lakes, which can be sailed along for weeks on end without returning once to the same place. Altogether, the Mazurian Lake District consists of 1370 lakes of more than one hectare in area.

Mazury is the greatest tourist attraction in Poland. The lakes are surrounded by a hilly post-glacial landscape formed by moraines, with vast meadows bathed in flowers. The local forests abound in wildlife (boar, elk, red deer and roe-deer, not to mention all kinds of small game). You will find old castles, isolated villages in the middle of the forest and other remote and mysterious places "where God lost his shoes".

Olsztyn is the main city of the Mazurian Lake District. It is the capital of Varmia, a historic region as closely tied with Mazury as Scotland with England. Varmia belonged to Poland for several centuries and remained Roman Catholic. Mazury was not an integral part of Poland, only a vassal province. Quite paradoxically the Mazurian people, the majority of whom were members of the Evangelical Church, stuck obsessively to the Polish speech. Maybe it was because they descended from some Mazovian settlers. Until recently, a few village communities of Mormons lived in Mazury.

Back in the past, at the beginning of the second millennium, Varmia and Mazury were inhabited not by Slavs, but by the Baltic tribes of Pruthenians and Sudovians, related to today's Lithuanians and Latvians. The Sudovians, a militant people constantly bothering their neighbours, were to be defeated and almost completely assimilated or killed off by the combined forces of the Teutonic Knights, Poles, Lithuanians and Ruthenians. The remainder were deported to distant lands, for instance to Mazovia. A few place names and surnames are now their only reminder. The Pruthenians, or Prussians, were Germanized. In exchange for that, their conquerors in knightly robes ornamented with a black cross had their state named Prussia. It developed into one of the strongest and most aggressive of all German states.

The medieval castle in Olsztyn is beautifully situated on the bank of the Łyna, near St. James's Cathedral and some fragments of the defensive walls. The castle once belonged to the chapter of the Teutonic Knights at Lidzbark Warmiński, where another huge castle is worth seeing. Olsztyn Castle was administered by Nicolaus Copernicus in the years 1515-21. As a true Renaissance man, he did not restrict his sphere of interest to astronomy. Among his many skills, including writing poetry, he was an efficient administrator and good economist. He formulated the law that "bad money drives out good" earlier than Gresham. He also proved to be a brilliant strategist, successfully defending the castle from the Teutonic Knights.

Today Olsztyn is far from being only a tourist attraction. It has a big tyre factory and the three adjacent lakes are not fit for bathing. But only several kilometres away the lakes are suitable not only for people but also for crayfish, creatures very sensitive to water pollution.

The most beautiful region, 100 kilometres east of Olsztyn, is called the "Land of Great Lakes". Śniardwy, Mamry, Bełdany, Niegocin, Roś and some smaller lakes together amount to 350 square kilometres of water surface. The main, well-equipped holiday centres are Mikołajki, Giżycko, Węgorzewo and Ruciane. Pleasure boats run from one lake port to another for those who prefer comfort rather than struggling with stays. Canoeing is most attractive on the enchanting meanders of the crystal clear River Krutynia.

What about some skiing? Snow stays long over the Mazurian land and its diversified topography provides ideal conditions for cross-country skiing. The Szeskie and Dylewskie Hills, more than 300 metres in height, offer good slopes for Alpine skiing, though perhaps not for ambitious skiers, while for iceboaters Mazury is a paradise.

A zoological curiosity, small wild forest horses are bred at Popielno on Lake Śniardwy in order to reproduce the species of tarpan, extinct since the 19th century.

Beavers, once close to extinction, now proliferate, driving the local farmers to despair, for the beavers' dams cause the flooding of their fields. Some muddy lakes provide habitat for a rare species of turtle.

The region west of Olsztyn, known as the Iława-Ostróda Lake District, has the large and twisted Lake Jeziorak as well as the interesting Elbląg Canal with its famous locks, where boats must be raised or lowered from one water level to the other. In the south of this region lies the village of Grunwald, where the most widely acclaimed battle with the Teutonic Knights took place in 1410. King Władysław Jagiełło and his cousin, Duke Witold of Lithuania, crushed the army

of the Grand Master Ulrich von Jungingen. Military historians have conducted thorough studies of this battle. Many strategic tricks used by King Władysław have been described, such as pretended escaping, flanking manoeuvres or using heavy cavalry in the decisive phase of the battle – all of them picked up by the king from the Tartars.

In the east, the Mazurian Lake District borders on to another lake district in the Suwałki region, in the distant past inhabited by the above mentioned Sudovians. According to many connoisseurs, this area of hilly land dotted with lakes on various heights, especially near Smolniki, is the most beautiful part of Poland. Perhaps they are right. Wigry being the most popular of the district's lakes, Hańcza is a natural wonder: the deepest lake in Poland (109 m) with elevated shores overgrown with forest. Through this lake flows the small river Czarna Hańcza, in its beauty surpassing even the famous Krutynia.

A local curiosity is the Orthodox Church community, who have been living in several local villages for three centuries. They continue to speak Old Russian and observe the strict principles of their faith. They marry within the community, though the young generation are now starting to break away. They never shave and they baptize their children by immersing them three times, head included, in cold water straight from a well.

A few thousand Lithuanians live near the town of Sejny and the village of Puńsk close to the Lithuanian border. They have their own schools and folk bands, and enjoy all the rights that ethnic minorities are entitled to.

The vast nearby Augustów Forest is also embellished with a series of beautiful lakes: Niecko, Białe, Studzieniczne, Sajno and the more distant Serwy. They are connected by natural passages and a canal with 18 sluices, built between 1825 and 1834. It was meant to form part of the route for exporting Polish goods to Windau (now Ventspils in Latvia) after the traditional route along the Vistula to Gdańsk had been cut off by the Prussian customs border. Later, when railways were introduced, water routes lost their importance. The canal was designed and its construction was supervised by General Ignacy Prądzyński, a great strategist who made a name for himself during the November Insurrection in 1830. Today the canal, no longer used for commercial purposes, is a precious historic monument of Polish engineering and also a wonderful route for water tourism.

The Mazurian Lakeland is a spellbinding region for lovers of water tourism.

Olsztyn. Freedom Square (Plac Wolności) with its early 20th century Town ▷
Hall built in a style that recalls the Baroque and Renaissance periods.

Miłomłyn and the extensive landscape of Varmian fields.

◁ *The Olsztyn Lakeland, where the forested shores of lakes encourage holiday rest and recreation.*

Ostróda is a centre for waterborne tourism. Pictured here is a jetty on Lake Drwęckie.

The Iława Lakeland forms a Landscape Park in which lakes
and forests are the dominant elements.

Żabi Róg is a Mazurian village not far from Morąg.

Bartoszyce was founded by the Teutonic Knights ▷
in the 14th century. Here we see the Gothic Lidzbark Gate.

*Lidzbark Warmiński, a seat of the Warmia Bishops
from the mid-14th century a Gothic castle on a square
plan with a courtyard and four corner towers.*

◁ *Sailing boats with set sails are a permanent
feature of the Mazurian Lakeland landscape.*

Święta Lipka, the Baroque Jesuit monastic complex. The Church of the Visitation of the Holy Virgin Mary; inside – a Baroque organ with movable parts.

The Borecka Forest boasts a wealth of old tree stands. ▷

Stańczyki. Poland's tallest viaduct carrying a now-disused railway line.

The sun can paint the landscape of Suwałki Landscape Park ▷
in this highly unsual way.

Suwałki Landscape Park and a view of Lakes Purwin,
Kojle and Perty. To be seen on the horizon is Góra Cisowa
– known as Suwałki's answer to Mount Fuji.

Lake Wigry is Poland's fifth deepest (reaching down to 73 m below ▷▷
the surrounding surface). Here the Camaldolite Monastery
and Church located picturesquely on a peninsula.

PODLASIE, THE BACKWOODS OF POLAND

Czarna Białostocka surrounded by Knyszyn Forest. An Orthodox church in the Buksztel district.

The first impression is "dark and wet", like in a primeval forest. And such a forest it is. The Białowieża Forest, the last great natural forest complex in Europe (outside Russia), has still some areas of virgin forest untouched by man. In the strict-reserve territory of the Białowieża National Park the lynx, wild boar, red deer and elk play host to visitors. The fauna sometimes includes a wolf or brown bear – illegally slipping across the "green border" with Belarus.

But the lord of the forest is the mighty bearded and horned European bison.

An average male of this splendid animal, weighing about a thousand kilograms, would make the American bison look like some weakling. The species became extinct after the First World War, having been killed for food. Not a single specimen was left in the Białowieża Forest, once its largest habitat. Fortunately for the bison, an international commission for its protection was set up with the active participation of Poland. Individual animals were purchased from various zoos – some of them were mixed with the Caucasian bison – and the researchers at Białowieża began to work on the restitution of the species. Today the number of bison in the Białowieża Forest amounts to 300, most of them living at liberty. As they were becoming short of space in the Białowieża Forest, some bison were transferred to other forests. The species has been saved and now the weaker specimens may even be hunted for – under the strict control of researchers and foresters and for a fat fee of tens of thousands dollars.

Białowieża National Park. In spring, the forest floor is carpeted with anemones.

The whole Białowieża Forest has an area of 1250 square kilometres, of which nearly 600 belong to Poland. The forest provides a natural research laboratory for all kinds of naturalists. It abounds in many species of ancient trees several centuries in age. Almost all the types of forest once covering the North European Plain have been preserved here.

Roaming the backwoods of Białowieża is by no means a safe and simple walk. It is quite an adventure, and a risky one unless you are an experienced hiker. Good orientation is needed not to get lost in the tangle of growing and fallen trees or get stuck in some boggy hollow. It may happen that an old rotten tree falls down all of a sudden with a bang. Wild, untamed nature! But if you meet a bison – do not panic. Even if it steps on the road to have a look at cars and people, it will soon with great dignity withdraw to the wood.

990 species of plants have been registered in the Białowieża Forest, not counting microflora.

The Białowieża Forest is a unique, pristine wilderness, whose greatest attraction is probably the European bison.

As many as 200 of these are lichens. Animal species number 11 000, three quarters of which are insects. 228 species of birds include the golden eagle, peregrine falcon, capercaillie and black grouse.

Another intact natural habitat, less known even to Poles, extends over the lowlands on the winding River Biebrza. The vast marshland, a true nature paradise, is now quite unique in Europe. Even elks like this wet terrain, and beavers seem to tolerate it, though muddy river banks are not their favourites. Before and after the Second World War the Biebrza Marshes were in danger of being drained by land reclamation engineers, bent on making every wet place dry. The Biebrza valley was lucky: the protracted argument between engineers and ecologists was won by the latter and the Biebrza National Park was established. Its unique character is marked by complete inaccessibility of the marshes and peatbogs in the autumn and spring. They can be entered neither on foot nor by boat. Countless pools, little canals and old river beds swarm with fish, but in order to go angling there it would be necessary to pass through treacherous swamps.

The whole Podlasie region is called "Poland B", which means inferior to the central and western parts of the country. It has poor, sandy soils, almost no industry and high unemployment. Not only its geographical situation, but also the local lifestyles and living standards place Podlasie closer to Belarus than to Central Europe. And a lot of Belorussians, mostly Orthodox, live in the vicinity of the Białowieża Forest.

They have their own holy hill, Grabarka, to which they make annual summer pilgrimages. They come from all directions carrying crosses – slightly different from the Roman Catholic ones – and chanting beautifully to God. It is one of the most mystic and exotic religious ceremonies performed in Poland.

With a bit of luck you may also hear a muezzin singing in this country. In the villages Bohoniki and Kruszyniany some descendants of King John III Sobieski's Tartar soldiers still bow down before Allah in their two historic mosques, reciting the verses of the Koran in the Arabic language they can no longer understand. Many more Tartars used to live in Poland before the Second World War. They even formed a Tartar cavalry squadron in the Polish army.

Ethnographers will perhaps take some interest in the so called "villages of the nobles" in the Podlasie region, inhabited by descendants of the minor landed gentry, equivalent to British yeomen. Although their life and wealth (or rather lack of it) at present is no different from that of their peasant neighbours, they are still proud of their noble origin, names and traditions. They boast their family coats of arms and swagger into the church on Sunday feeling better than the rest of the villagers. About sixty years or so ago it could still happen that a Podlasie nobleman ploughed his field carrying his curved sword strapped to his waist. In more recent times, his daughters had to wear gloves when pulling up weeds in the flowerbeds or milking cows. Maybe they still do?

Where there is nobility, there are horses. The stud-farm at Janowiec Podlaski has been keeping thoroughbred Arab horses for nearly two hundred years. Millionaires from all over the world attend its horse auctions every year.

The rural character of the Podlasie region is a tourist attraction in itself, for such pristine landscapes are hardly seen any more in modern and rich areas. Białystok, the main city of the region, has expanded in the last decades. This otherwise commonplace city has one gem: the Branicki Palace designed by Tylman van Gameren in the 18th century. One of the most beautiful Baroque palaces in Poland, it is locally called "the Podlasie Versailles". Not without reason: among the guests of the Branicki family were some members of the royal Bourbon family who managed to escape the Jacobinic guillotine. Today the palace houses the Medical Academy.

Admirers of old architecture, especially post-modernists bored with modern designs, will like the small town of Tykocin. Picturesquely situated on the River Narew far from the main roads, it is said to be a sleepy place where dogs are too lazy to bark and cats sleep on window sills instead of straying. The Baroque Church and Monastery of the Missionaries, the beautifully restored synagogue and the 17th century almshouse for disabled soldiers, probably the first in Poland, create an olden-times aura aroud Tykocin. Time seems to have stopped here.

Apart from Białystok, two other smaller cities, Siedlce and Łomża, aspire to becoming the main cities of the Podlasie region.

Siedlce belonged to the famous aristocratic Czartoryski family. They built a Neo-Classical palace, later passed to another great family, the Ogińskis. Two fine parks: a landscaped and a geometric one have survived from the aristocratic times. And that is all – too little for an important town.

Łomża, beautifully situated on the high Narew escarpment, looks more interesting. It used to be one of the major towns in Mazovia. Once bigger than Warsaw, it was a bishop's seat, with a late-Gothic cathedral, later rebuilt in the Baroque style. Huge fortifications dating from the tsarist times are a great attraction for fans of military architecture.

The marshland along the Narew, which spreads for some fifty miles, is a bird sanctuary and has recently become a national park.

Hajnówka, a village at the outskirts of Białowieża Forest.
The modern Orthodox Church of the Holy Trinity.

Topiło is a small lake on the edge ▷
of the Białowieża Forest.

Tykocin is a smallish town on the Narew. Its Baroque-style
synagogue is now a Jewish Museum.

Białowieża Forest, part of the Białowieża National Park ▷▷
designated by UNESCO as a Biosphere Reserve.

The Siemianowski Reservoir, an artificial lake on the Narew.

The Narew. Flood waters of the unregulated river.

Grabarka is the most famous shrine of the Orthodox Church in Poland. ▷
The crosses of penitence were brought here by the faithful.

The River Biebrza and its tributaries create extensive floodlands in spring. The National Park established here protects rare flora and fauna, as well as the unique natural landscape of the floodplain.

The Biebrza marshes. The Biebrza National Park, ▷ a unique natural reserve in Europe.

◁ Lake Rajgrodzkie in the Ełk Lakeland.

Ciechanowiec. Skansen museum of wooden folk architecture.

Białystok. The Baroque Palace of the Branicki Family is situated in a large landscaped park known as the "Versailles of Podlasie". Here the grand stairway.

The Biebrza River meanders through fens ▷▷ and overgrown marshes.

Złaków Kościelny. The Corpus Christi Procession with the colourful folk costume of the Łowicz region.

Mazovia region. A characteristic landscape with willow in flower.

Warsaw. The Mermaid of the Old Town is but one representation of this aquatic symbol of Warsaw, which features on the city's coat of arms.

MAZOVIA, THE LAND OF CHOPIN

Warsaw's coat of arms depicts a mermaid – a half-beautiful woman, half-fish. The hybrid raises her sword to some enemy. It is a suitable emblem for a city called "Invincible". Warsaw is rather ugly, with some beautiful places; a hybrid which has always been very rebellious.

Its ugliness is an effect of the conglomeration of districts completely unmatched with one another. The city lacks any imposing structures except for the Palace of Culture and Science, built for Warsaw by Stalin's order as a gift from the "fraternal Soviet nation". This massive tower in the very centre of the city, a replica of its many Moscow prototypes, would provoke many jokes and cause general disgust. Varsovians call it "the dream of a drunk confectioner", as the construction resembles a gigantic wedding cake.

Warsaw was destroyed almost every century. In the 17th century the town was ruined by the Swedish invasion, known as "the Deluge". The Russian General Suvorov perpetrated a massacre in the Praga district on the right bank of the Vistula at the end of the 18th century. The town suffered from the Russians under General Paskevitch when they crushed the November Insurrection in 1831. The First World War did not inflict serious damage on Warsaw, but the Second World War nearly wiped out the city with four waves of destruction. The disaster started in September 1939, when Warsaw defended itself from the Nazi forces in complete isolation for three weeks. Then in 1943 the Germans put down the desperate Jewish Ghetto Uprising and completely erased their entire district. Then came the main Polish uprising in August and September 1944, known as the Warsaw Uprising, but the final destruction did not come until after the almost complete evacuation of the main, left bank and Hitler's insane order that no trace of the city should remain.

When the Soviet Army entered Warsaw to secure power for the communists, the city practically did not exist. It was even planned to transfer the capital to Łódź. But the overwhelming feeling was that only Warsaw, a symbol of patriotism and bravery, could be the capital of Poland. So the reconstruction of the historic district of the Old Town and the Royal Way was started and it soon yielded results.

The old quarters were brought back to their original, or even greater, splendour. As most of the blueprints were lost during the war, the designers and builders had to use old photographs and even the paintings of Bernardo Bellotto, called Canaletto, a great 18th century painter of Warsaw views. In a few years patina covered the Old Town houses and nobody in Warsaw cares that they are only half a century old.

The later decades brought pseudo-modern methods of building, such as large-panel construction. Huge, dull and featureless housing developments of blocks of flats were built in the outskirts of Warsaw, like in many other cities in Europe.

Nevertheless, some fragments of Warsaw could well belong to the most elegant of cities. Take for instance Krakowskie Przedmieście. The wide, artistically irregular street starts from Zamkowy (Castle) Square, where the soaring Sigismund III Vasa Column, another symbol of Warsaw, commemorates the ruler who transferred the capital from Cracow to Warsaw four centuries ago. Krakowskie Przedmieście is lined with mostly neoclassical but also some Baroque palaces and almost exclusively Baroque churches. Starting from the monument of the king who "moved the capital", the street ends at the monument of the astronomer who "moved the Earth" – Nicolaus Copernicus. Here in the first place. It is a pity that the U.S. Embassy building, an ordinary glass and concrete construction, so utterly fails to match the surrounding parks and palaces.

Apart from the route known as the Royal Way, linking the Renaissance Royal Castle with neoclassical Belvedere, Warsaw has very few imposing buildings. There is the Grand Theatre, a masterpiece of neoclassicism designed by Antonio Corazzi, some fine churches, and of course the Old Town Market Square with the streets around it. Each of its houses, once owned by the Warsaw patricians, is charming, and each differs from the rest. The Gothic intermingles with the Renaissance and the Baroque, history with legend. The monster which inhabited the cellars of the Basilisk House killed people with its stare until it was approached with a mirror and killed itself. Each house has a name, e.g. The Crocodile or Baryczka, and each of them is connected with some memory. Here the shoemaker Jan Kiliński prepared his rebellion, while over there lived Maria Skłodowska-Curie. Another one houses the Museum of Literature dedicated to Adam Mickiewicz (who never even visited Warsaw). Still another – the Historical Museum of Warsaw. Next to it the Fukier wine cellar, where it has been hard to find a vacant place for three hundred years.

It is impossible to list all museums, but the National Museum, situated up the Vistula escarpment off the Royal Way, is of prime importance. It has a splendid gallery of Polish painting and rich collections of foreign art.

Warsaw has some nice parks, including one on a European scale: Łazienki Park. It was designed in English style with some French elements, like the section around the Chopin Monument with a weeping willow over it. The park, arranged on a steep slope of the escarpment, is characterized by magnificent old trees, dense shrubbery and a chain of ponds. A number of fine buildings gracefully complement the natural landscape. The Palace on the Water, a favourite residence of the last Polish king, Stanisław Augustus Poniatowski, is a perfect combination of Baroque and neoclassicism, known as the "King Stanisław style". The design was made by the famous architect Domenico Merlini according to the king's own ideas. The Old Orangery used to house one of the oldest theatres in Europe. The Summer Theatre on the Island is a replica of an ancient amphitheatre. A lot of other buildings are hidden amid the greenery. When feeling tired, a visitor may rest on a bench and enjoy the company of friendly park squirrels.

Some insist, however, that the Ignacy Paderewski (or Skaryszew) Park in Praga district is even more beautiful than Łazienki. The English park, ornamented with hills, clusters of old trees, ponds and lush meadows, is a green oasis in the middle of a busy city.

As to the old districts of Warsaw, they must have once been very beautiful, something which is reflected by the names of those former aristocratic quarters. Since in old times all fashions came from Paris, the names were derived from French. The present Mokotów has originated from Mon Coteau, that is "my hill", as the oldest part of the district stretched over the Warsaw escarpment. Marymont is the French for Mount of Mary. Żoliborz, before the last war a district of army officers and rich intelligentsia, has been coined from Joli bord, or "beautiful bank" (of the Vistula). The river has in the meantime moved away from Żoliborz, leaving a wide stretch of meadows, good for walking along or horse riding. The Baroque palace-cum-garden complex at Wilanów, former village, now within the city limits, is certainly worth a visit. Here King John III Sobieski resided with his beloved Queen Marie-Casimire, in Polish just Marysieńka. Today Wilanów is a branch of the National Museum. From time to time a royal visitor to Poland happens to reside in the palace.

At the other end of the outskirts of Warsaw stretches the Kampinos Forest, 225 square kilometres of which constitute the Kampinos National Park. It is rare that such a splendid, natural forest habitat is found so close to a great metropolis.

Outside the north edge of the Kampinos Forest, the widely flowing Vistula is joined by its largest tributaries, the Bug and Narew. These two rivers are treated as one, because geographers are unable to decide which of them flows into the other. The Bug is evidently longer, for it starts as far away as Ukraine, while the Narew carries more water, gathered in the Podlasie and Mazury regions.

Anyway, the Vistula swells when they join it at the foot of the Modlin fortress, built and extended from the time of Napoleon Bonaparte till the Second World War.

In 1939 the defenders of Modlin continued to fight till the very end in support of besieged Warsaw. Going down the river we arrive at Zakroczym, a town dating back to the Piast times. In 1831 it served for a week as a provisional capital of Poland, for when the November Insurrection had fallen, an army of thirty-thousand under General Maciej Rybiński was still stationed at Zakroczym. From here they marched to Prussia and then to France, to the "Great Emigration". Today Zakroczym is known as the capital of the greatest onion farming region in Poland.

At Czerwińsk, further down the Vistula, the 12th century monastery church has survived, where Bishop Albert of Paris settled a group of French monks. This points to the fact that travel between Poland and France was not only one-way. Inside the church, some Romanesque wall paintings were uncovered. They document the early stage of development of French painting: the saints have big heads with circular halos round them and wings resembling Indian headdress. The paintings are considered by art historians to be extremely precious.

At this spot the great army of King Władysław Jagiełło crossed the Vistula on its way to Grunwald. The soldiers built a half-kilometre long bridge over the river supported on boats. It was a wonder of medieval military engineering. The Teutonic Knights' commander refused to believe his own scouts reporting that the Poles "built a bridge in the air", and he did not bother to concentrate all his units. As a result, he lost his life and the whole of his army.

Not far from Czerwińsk is another wonder of civil engineering: the longest wooden bridge in Europe, or maybe in the whole world, at Wyszogród. It has 60 spans and 1250 metres. Every few years, when the water in the spring gets dangerously high and carries huge ice-floes, the whole country is alarmed if the bridge will withstand the pressure this time. But somehow it is always saved by brave sappers.

There are some picturesque islands on the Vistula beyond Wyszogród. Apart from providing breeding sites for gulls, terns and other birds, including some rare species, they serve as pastures for cattle.

On the right, high bank of the Vistula emerges the beautiful skyline of Płock. Most of the historic relics in Płock lie on Tumskie Hill: the 12th century Cathedral with soaring towers, fragments of a medieval castle and the former Benedictine Abbey. Today Płock is the centre of the Polish petrochemical industry.

The environs of Warsaw are not particularly attractive. They are as flat as a pancake and built up with ugly suburbia. It must have looked different in the past, when young Frédéric Chopin fell in love with the idyllic Mazovian countryside. The composer's heart rests in an urn fixed into the wall of the Holy Cross Church in Warsaw, though his grave is in the Pere Lachaise cemetery in Paris.

Chopin was born in a small manor-house at Żelazowa Wola near Warsaw. It has survived and now houses a museum devoted to the composer. Concerts of Chopin's music are performed there regularly, to the great applause of music lovers from various countries.

A little further away from Warsaw stands the imposing Nieborów Palace, also designed by Tylman van Gameren. It was the residence of Primate Radziejowski, then of the Ogiński family and finally – the famous Polish-Lithuanian family of the Radziwiłłs.

Nearby Łowicz is famous for the most beautiful folk costumes. They are still worn by the Łowicz women on such occasions as the Corpus Christi procession. This colourful event always attracts thousands of tourists.

Warsaw. Freta Street. To be seen in the background is the Pauline Church of the Holy Ghost. ▷
Warsaw. A panorama of the Old Town from across the Vistula. ▷▷

◁ Warsaw. The Royal Castle as seen
from Świętojańska Street.

Warsaw. The Throne Room is one of the Royal Castle's richest
and most beautiful rooms.

Warsaw. The Old Town was more or less reduced to rubble during the Second
World War, but was rebuilt painstakingly. Piwna Street is to be seen here.

Krakowskie Przedmieście Street as seen ▷▷
from Warsaw's Castle Square.

Warsaw. Modernity contrasts with old architecture on Krasiński Square, with its Field Cathedral to the Polish Army and new Supreme Court building.

Warsaw. The fifties-style Palace of Culture and Science ▷ has become its own unique kind of tourist attraction.

Warsaw. The enclosed courtyard to the main building of Warsaw Technical University (or Polytechnic) which was established at the initiative of Stanisław Staszic in 1825.

The modern architecture of Warsaw's city centre, ▷▷ as seen along Jana Pawła II Avenue.

Warsaw. The Łazienki Park and Palace complex
with its neo-Classical Palace on the Island.

Warsaw. The Palace on the Island with its subtly-sculpted
Grand Ballroom.

Warsaw. Wilanów, on the city's southern edge, boasts one of the finest ▷
magnate's residences in Poland. Here we see the front elevation of the palace,
which was summer home to King Jan III Sobieski (reigning 1674-1696).

Warsaw, Wilanów Palace. The Grand Crimson Room is furnished with a gigantic table.
It is here that the official receptions took place.

Natolin is now within Warsaw. Its 18th century palace, remodelled in the Neo-Classical style – stands in a landscaped park.

Petrykozy. A 19th century Neo-Classical manor house with a collection of folk art assembled by Wojciech Siemion.

Ojrzanów. A landscaped park by the 19th century Palace. ▷

Pułtusk stands on the Narew and is known as "Mazovia's Venice". The old Castle of the Bishops of Płock is now the Dom Polonia.

Kobyłka is a small locality near Warsaw. The Late Baroque church boasts a Rococo altarin the shape of a modified tabernacle.

Liw lies on the boundary between the Mazovia and Podlasie regions. Here the gate tower of the old Castle of the Dukes of Mazovia plus Baroque-style manor.

◁ *Goźlin, a village in the middle Vistula valley. Interior of the wooden Baroque church.*

Zielonka near Warsaw attests to the fact that some charming and quiet corners are still to be found near even the biggest and busiest cities.

Treblinka. A symbolic cemetery, wherein some 17,000 boulders pay homage to those ▷ murdered in the extermination camp set up by the Nazis. Among those to die here was the famous orphanage founder and teacher Janusz Korczak.

Sierpc. The Museum of the Mazovian Countryside brings together old farmsteads, chapels and farming implements on a 60 ha site.

Łyse is a centre for the folk art and culture ▷ of the Kurpie region. Regional folk ensembles perform here.

◁ Czerwińsk on the Vistula, a former centre of river trade. Monastery with the Romanesque Parish Church.

Brudzeński Landscape Park is by the Vistula, not far from Płock. Its main attractions are its beautiful forests.

Żelazowa Wola, the birthplace of Frédéric Chopin. The Chopin family's manor-house.

Brochów boasts a Gothic-Renaissance fortified church in which Frederic Chopin was baptized.

Nieborów Palace, containing the painting gallery and ancient sculpture collection founded in the 18th. century.

Zaborów. The eclectic palace of Leon Goldstand ▷ dates back to the beginning of the 20th century.

Oporów. The Gothic Knights' Castle built of brick in a square shape, surrounded by a moat and park.

Złaków is a small village in which the traditions of the Łowicz region are nurtured. ▷ Here the return home after the Corpus Christi procession.

The Vistula in Mazovia region – the wide, unregulated queen of Poland's rivers. ▷▷

THE POLISH MANCHESTER

Łódź and its Księży Młyn industrial district. The Central Room of the Palace of Edward Herbst, which is a museum featuring interiors from the mansions of late 19th and early 20th century Łódź industrialists.

The Łódż region. Work in the fields at potato harvest time.

Sulejów. St. Benedict and his followers as sculpted in the capitulary of the Cistercian Monastery.

The Sieradz-Łęczyca land merges with the Łódź region, which has developed over the last two centuries. Before, there was no such region, though the little village of Łodzia came into being during the 14th century. It was even granted a town charter in 1423, but hardly anyone had heard about it in Poland until the 19th century. In 1820 it had only 767 inhabitants and after a few decades – five hundred times more. Łódź not only emerged rapidly, but it soon became the second-biggest city in Poland, its population now amounting to one million.

A major causal factor was the invention of mechanical, initially steam-driven spinning and weaving. The first factory in Łódź, today housing the Textile Industry Museum, was built by a Mr Ludwik Geyer in 1835-37. Other businessmen followed his example and in a short time Łódź was labelled a "Polish Manchester". The 19th century producers took advantage of the absence of a customs border between the Russian Empire and its partition zone called the Kingdom of Poland and they sold their fabrics to the entire tsarist empire as far as the Pacific.

Polish capitalism – or rather Polish, immigrant German, Russian and Jewish – developed in Łódź. For many decades it was a cosmopolitan and rich city; rich but unsightly. It was built up chaotically, shabbily and too densely. No attention was paid to aesthetics or basic conveniences. Łódź has been undergoing renovation for fifty years now, but it is still a gloomy city, even though the infrastructure has been greatly improved.

Obviously, you would not expect to find any historic sights in a city like this. But what has not so far been regarded as a historic place may become so one day. This is going to happen to Piotrkowska Street. The unique, extremely long thoroughfare is lined with Art Nouveau houses. Some of the palaces in which the first tycoons resided, fenced off with high walls from unpleasant factory and workers' quarters, have now gained the status of historic monuments. As the fin de siecle is again in fashion, more and more people in Łódź are finding their city beautiful.

The cultural circles in Łódź can take pride in at least two of the city's institutions: the Museum of Modern Art, boasting the richest collection of avant-garde painting in Poland, and the only Polish Higher School of Cinema, Theatre and TV. It was from this school that the world famous "Polish film school" emerged in the 1950s and 1960s. Such great artists as Andrzej Wajda, Andrzej Munk, Wojciech Has, Krzysztof Zanussi, Roman Polański

Łódź is a city whose flowering came in the mid 19th century, as the textile industry developed. In this photo, Freedom Square (Plac Wolności) with its Monument to Tadeusz Kościuszko, Church of the Holy Spirit and former Town Hall from the 19th century.

and Krzysztof Kieślowski made their films for the Łódź film company.

Piotrków Trybunalski, a close neighbour of Łódź, was famous before anyone had heard a word about Łódź. It was first mentioned in written records in 1217. The Gothic Parish Church and the Dominican Monastery date back to the 14th century. Many other sacred and secular buildings were erected in the Renaissance and Baroque periods, when the nobility gathered in the town for general and provincial assemblies. For nearly three centuries until the partitions of Poland, Piotrków was a seat of the Crown Tribunal, which settled the disputes from Mazovia and Wielkopolska. Piotrków inhabitants are very proud of their past and they are sorry now that their town is becoming a satellite of the nearby Bełchatów. No one knew Bełchatów until brown coal started to be extracted here. Miners have already dug a huge hollow in the ground – certainly the largest in Poland – and are making it larger and larger. The coal

is used to produce electricity supply for one-fifth of Poland.

The "greater Łódź" area is surrounded by a number of small towns with a developed textile industry, such as Zduńska Wola, Zgierz, Pabianice, Aleksandrów and others. They have not much to offer to tourists, but on the other hand... At Pabianice there are a few traces of the Renaissance style and some old wooden houses from the early 19th century. In the Blue Springs nature reserve near Tomaszów Mazowiecki karst springs flow out profusely. Skierniewice has the famous Institute of Fruit-growing, where new and tasty apple varieties are being grown. Halfway between Łódź and Warsaw, at Radziejowice (the former Radziejowski), the Krasiński Palace today serves as a creative work centre for artists, writers and scientists. It is also a favourite place for the secret meetings of freemasons.

Łódź. Piotrkowska Street, the city's main thoroughfare, stretches for 4km, and is regarded as Europe's longest commercial street.

Łódź features the late 19th and early 20th century Neo-Baroque mansion of industrialist Izrael Poznański. In this view, the garden side. ▷

Łódź. The fine Dining Room in Izrael Poznański's Mansion.

Łódź. The Mauretanian Room in the mansion of Karol Scheibler from the second half of the 19th century. The mansion now houses a Museum of Cinematography.

Zgierz, a centre of the textile industry. ▷ View of the church from the early 20th century.

Piotrków Trybunalski was once seat to the Crown Tribunal. The Jesuit Collegiate Church and Baroque Church of St. Francis Xavier.

Radziejowice. 17th century palace connected with a small castle, rebuilt in the 19th century.

Żyrardów is a textile town which grew up in the 19th century. It was the site of Poland's first strike in 1883.

◁ Sulejów. The Late Romanesque Cistercian Monastery complex with St. Thomas's Church erected from blocks of sandstone plus bricks.

The Łódź region, with plantations of sunflowers ▷▷ extending to the horizon.

Sieradz. The folk tradition is preserved here as young people take pride in their regional costumes.

The miraculous likeness of the Licheń Mother of God.

Spicimierz celebrates Corpus Christi.

KALISZ WAS KNOWN TO PTOLEMY

Most of the oldest towns in Poland were founded about a thousand years ago, when the Polish state was formed by the Piasts. According to archaeological studies, there were some exceptions founded much earlier.

Kalisz is an exception among exceptions.
It was mentioned as "Kalisia" (not "Calisia" as many historians report) by Ptolemy of Alexandria himself in the 2nd century A.D. Kalisia was one of 8,000 localities on the map of the world included in his work on geographical learning, which was not available to Europeans until the 15th century, when it was already out-of-date.

The name "Kalisia" was recorded at the time when the Roman empire was threatened by Germanic tribes and the Parthians. It became necessary to watch the barbarian lands across the Danube and the Rhine more closely. What that "Kalisia" actually was is not clear. That it was a camp or a station of the Roman legions sounds improbable. It might have been an open trade settlement on the old Amber Route. But it cannot be ruled out that it was the centre of a small tribe of Kalisians mentioned as "Helisians" by Tacitus even earlier than Ptolemy.

Unfortunately, archaeologists have not found any traces of that ancient Kalisia at Kalisz. The findings date back to no earlier than the 9th century.
One of them is the oldest beehive excavated in Poland. It has been preserved together with a honeycomb, one of those which made our forefathers' lives sweet.

At the beginning of the second millennium Kalisz developed into the seat of a little provincial duchy. Many buildings have survived from that and later times – from the Gothic to the neoclassical period.
They add a patina to the town, a rather dignified and old-fashioned look. Otherwise Kalisz has no particularly valuable historic relics. The greatest damages were inflicted on old Kalisz architecture at the beginning of the First (not Second) World War, as in most other Polish towns.

A highly valuable historic building is the mid-12th century Romanesque Collegiate Church at Tum.
The village was once the central part of Łęczyca, numbered among the oldest towns in Poland, the first settlement there dating to the 6th century. Art historians find many analogies between the Tum church and the Romanesque religious architecture in Rhineland, Lorraine and even Normandy.

The Łęczyca and the neighbouring Sieradz lands lie in the very centre of Poland, where the three historic

Kalisz is a town whose history stretches back to Roman times. Here the Baroque Collegiate Church of the Assumption of the Blessed Virgin Mary and St. Joseph.

regions of Wielkopolska, Mazovia and Małopolska meet. The region should be of interest for those who pursue linguistic studies on the Polish language. Local country people speak almost a literary language, with very little dialectic traits. Other specialists who may like this region are probably... demonologists. The most famous of Polish devils, called Boruta, Rokita and some other local names, prowled in the area. He was imagined as an elegant nobleman in traditional attire, although what he liked best was roaming the forests and swamps.

Sieradz, a town on the Warta as old as Łęczyca, was described by the 12th century Arab traveller al-Idrisi as one of the biggest towns in Poland. A Piast duke resided here and important political rallies of the nobility took place, as well as synods of bishops. No imposing munuments of architecture are found in Sieradz beside the Dominican monastery and church from the 14th century. Instead, the cultural folk heritage of the region – much revered and still alive in some villages – has been preserved in the skansen of the Ethnographic Park.

North of Kalisz, halfway to Kruszwica on the ancient trail known as the Roman Amber Route, near the town of Konin, you will find a stone pillar, which is hardly ever noticed though it is probably one of the oldest

preserved proto-Slavic or maybe even Celtic figural sculptures. Whether it represented a monk or a bear cannot be told now that time has blurred its contours. When no longer needed – for its loss of quality or the people's change of faith – around the 12th century it was turned into a road post. And so it stands.

Is there anyone who still cares about some old piece of stone when a new vibrant industrial centre is developing around, based on brown coal extracted for the local power plant from several opencast mines in the vicinity? The cooling water from the plant is poured out very hot into the nearby lakes. As a result, some stenothermal fish species which have never before occurred in Poland have appeared in these lakes.

North of Konin beyond the Grąblin forest, the towers of St. Mary's Sanctuary are seen from a distance in the village of Stary Licheń. The holy site is visited by hundreds of thousands of tourists. A man-made hill called Golgotha is quite a unique sight.

The rural landscape of the Sieradz region.

Ożarów – Baroque manor-house.
Museum of Manor Interiors, Hunters' Room.

The Szachownica ("Chessboard") Cave near Wieluń. ▷

Spicimierz. The Corpus Christi processional route is carpeted with flowers.

Licheń Stary. An idyllic landscape with a country road. ▷

The Sieradz folk ensemble in the regional skansen museum. ▷▷

*Tum near Łęczyca. 12th century Romanesque
Collegiate Church.*

*The Konin area boasts a great many lakes, by which
the city people find rest and recreation at weekends.*

The Konin region. Potato harvest. ▷

Łęczyca. The Castle here is associated with the legendary devil Boruta, so the Courtyard has proved a good place to display folk carvings of imps and other figures from the dark side.

Sieradz. Folk sculpture in the skansen museum.

◁ The Łęczyca area and wintertime forest.

The Pątnów power station. Industry took root
in the picturesque country side of the Konin area.

A romantic sunset in the Uniejów area. ▷
A frozen winter landscape near Licheń Stary, a small village not far from Konin. ▷▷

THE CRADLE OF POLES

The species Homo sapiens arrived relatively late in the Polish lands, discouraged for thousands of years by severe climatic conditions. It was cold here during the four successive glacial periods, the last of which ended some 10,000 years ago. Only then did the warmer Holocene, or present epoch, start.

It was therefore a long time before any man appeared in this land or left any definite traces. If he had made some attempts to settle in Poland before the last glaciation, it must have been somewhere in the south of the country in the mountain foothills. It was not until some 8,000 years B.C. that fine forests started to grow all over Poland and palaeolithic man arrived with his quarry stone tools. He knew how to make a bow and could hunt for reindeer. He preferred to settle near water, and thus kept advancing towards the neolithic era. When it came, he replaced his flaked stone tools with ground stone ones. He bred goats, pigs and cattle and sowed various crops, becoming more and more civilized.

Where he came from is not certain. Perhaps from the Danube. Years, centuries and millennia passed. The inhabitants of the present Poland, or – to be precise – its part called "Great Poland" (Wielkopolska), already believed in the afterlife and built sizeable mounds (some of them longer than a hundred metres) to their deceased. As fashions in pottery changed, clay pots were shaped into funnel beakers or spherical amphorae, then string- or stroke-ornamented and the like. The people probably spoke proto-Indo-European, from which many names have survived, such as the rivers Wisła (Vistula) and Odra (Oder).

Step by step, the Lusatian culture developed, evidently Slavic, though not yet Polish. Among a great number of its relics, the best known is the fortified settlement of Biskupin. It had 13 parallel streets encircled by a rampart with a palisade and was inhabited by around 1,000 people. For safety, it was built on a lake island, which has now turned into a peninsula. It all took place about twenty-five centuries ago, that is two centuries ab urbe condita (from the foundation of Rome). The Biskupin settlement was discovered in 1933 and has been partly reconstructed in its archaic shape as a relic from the early Iron Age.

It took over a thousand years more – stormy years, marked by many migrations of peoples through this land – before the Polish state began to develop from the tribe of Polanes.

The first legendary ruler of the Polanes was a simple wheelwright (or a ploughman as other legends say), whose son, Siemowit, defeated Popiel the ruler of Gniezno. According to other legends, Popiel lived

In Strzelno, the Church of the Holy Trinity features this carved Romanesque column.

Ląd. The monumental Cistercian monastery complex with its two-towered Baroque church.

Pyzdry. A recently-uncovered fresco in the monastery from the 14th-18th centuries.

at Kruszwica on Lake Gopło and was finally devoured by mice. The famous Mouse Tower preserved at Kruszwica, where it is all said to have taken place, was in fact built several centuries later. Whatever, the Piast rulers Siemowit, Leszek and Siemomysł are believed to have united a few small tribes into one big tribe of Polanes, defeated their neighbours, the Goplanes, and brought Duke Mieszko I to the world. He united (or conquered) other Polish tribes, married the Bohemian Duchess Dobravka and was baptized in 966, thus advancing on the way to Europe.

Gniezno was then the capital of Poland. Before, it might have been a little island settlement on Lake Lednica, called Ostrów Lednicki, where the remains of some pre-Romanesque stone buildings have survived, possibly the oldest in Poland. Bolesław the Brave, son of Mieszko I and the first crowned king of Poland, liked to stay in Gniezno. His second favourite town was Poznań, where the first bishopric was established in 968. It was subordinated directly to Rome, which suggests that the "Land of Mieszko" (the name "Poland" came into use in later times) was from the very beginning treated as a politically independent state. Even greater favour was bestowed on Gniezno in 1000: it became an archbishops' seat. The honour of being the religious centre of Poland has been enjoyed by the town to this day.

Gniezno Cathedral, built in the Gothic style in the years 1342-72, contains an earlier, extremely valuable masterpiece of Romanesque art: the bronze doors with bas-relief, cast probably by masters from Lorraine. The doors depict the life of St. Adalbert, a Bohemian missionary to pagan Prussia killed there in 997. Relics of the saint – one of Poland's patrons – are kept in the Cathedral. The greatest statesmen of the Middle Ages, including the martyr's personal friend Emperor Otto III, came to pay respect to the relics. The Emperor presented King Bolesław with the diadem and spear of St. Maurice as a symbol of Polish sovereignty.

The present capital of Wielkopolska, Poznań, is a much bigger and more interesting town than Gniezno. The Cathedral on Ostrów Tumski (once an island on the Warta) was built as a pre-Romanesque basilica. In the 11th century it was extended and remodelled in the Romanesque and then in the Gothic style. Later styles – the Renaissance, Baroque and neoclassicism – also had some impact on its decoration. The Golden Chapel, the mausoleum of the Polish state founders Mieszko I and Bolesław the Brave, was rebuilt in the romantic Byzantine style at the beginning of the 19th century. The walls of this ancient cathedral combined nearly all styles ever flourishing in the Polish land. Alas, it was severely damaged during the fighting in 1945, and it was reconstructed in its Gothic shape, with fragments of the oldest foundations preserved in the crypt.

Poznań has many other historic buildings: the beautiful Gothic Church of the Holy Virgin Mary, with fine polychrome painting and stained glass by contemporary painter Taranczewski, the Baroque Parish Church and the Town Hall, a masterpiece of the Renaissance, which could well have been transplanted from the Italian peninsula.

Compared to other Polish cities, Poznań is thought to be a reliable place with earnest and hard-working people, a wealthy city, but in the eyes of Varsovians and Cracovians a little dull and unimaginative. This may be a false opinion resulting from the fact that Poznań was the main city of the Prussian partition zone for over a hundred years. It may have absorbed some of the German life style, but at heart it has always remained earnestly and passionately a Polish city. When Poland was recreating itself after the First World War, the Poznań inhabitants organized a victorious uprising against the Germans. They were the first to rebel against the Stalinist regime in 1956. Although their rebellion was suppressed with bloodshed by the communists, it initiated underground resistance in Poland. At times weaker or completely put down, the movement exploded in 1980 in Gdańsk, as the Solidarity under Lech Wałęsa. The Poznań events in 1956 also ignited the revolt in Budapest, which ended in the tragic massacre in the city by the Red Army.

The environs of Poznań and the whole Wielkopolska region are characterized by a plain, flat landscape. The only diversity is given to it by some lakes, especially Lake Gopło, enshrouded in legend, and the forests of the Wielkopolska National Park. Local villages are famous for their economy rather than for scenic views. Still, the landscape is diversified by some magnates' palaces, now used as museums. The Baroque-neoclassical Raczyński Palace at Rogalin is known for its fine interiors, the gallery of paintings, and above all for the famous "Rogalin oaks" of imposing size (the greatest of them is 9 metres in circumference) and quantity (their number amounts to nearly one thousand). The 16th century castle of the Działyński family at Kórnik contains historical art collections and interesting archaeological and mineral finds, also from outside Poland, as well as a library of 150,000 volumes, including many priceless old editions. The last owner of the castle, Władysław Zamoyski, offered the castle and all collections as a gift to the Polish nation. The castle park extends into a vast parkland arranged in the Italian, French and English styles from the early 19th century.

As far as sacred buildings are concerned, the early-12th century Romanesque Collegiate Church at Kruszwica is not only very old, but also exceptionally pure in style. The rotunda of St. Procopius and Holy Trinity Church, which form part of the monastery complex of the Premonstratensian nuns at Strzelno, are not much younger. Unusually beautiful and rare

Zielona Góra, the capital of the Lubusz Land, known for its vine harvest festival.

Romanesque figural sculptures have been preserved inside the church.

The tradition of fairs in Poznań dates back to the 15th century. The annual Poznań International Fair was highly renowned among traders in the period between the two World Wars. Since 1973 general trade fairs and industrial fairs have been held separately.

The Leszno and Lubusz lands belong to Wielkopolska, as well as the small region of Pałuki, whose rich folk culture has been preserved, and an interesting area around the towns of Śmigiel and Osieczna, where the windmills standing on hills make the landscape look like the Spanish province of La Mancha.

Leszno, a town bordering on the region of Silesia, was owned by the Wieniawa family, later renamed Leszczyński – prominent aristocrats. In the 16th century Leszno became a scientific, cultural and publishing centre of the Bohemian and Moravian Brethren, who escaped to Poland from persecution in their homeland. Their leader and rector of the local university was the famous pedagogue and philosopher Jan Amos Komenský, who later in his life continued his activity based on the teachings of Jan Huss in Amsterdam. Leszno has a number of precious Baroque structures, like the Town Hall finely rebuilt by Pompeo Ferrari. The Baroque palace at Rydzyna belonged to the families of Leszczyński and then Sułkowski – the founders of the once excellent Piarist Academy.

The Lubusz region, named after the frontier town now in Germany and called Lebus, has two rivalling cities: Zielona Góra and Gorzów. It is also characterized by much more diversified landscape full of forests and lakes. At Łagów, the beautiful 14th century castle of the Knights of Malta standing on an isthmus between two lakes attracts the "best society" of film makers, at whose events guests are treated with the local wine, made of grapes grown in the vicinity of Zielona Góra.

Wielkopolska is a region rich in extensive forest complexes. ▷
Gniezno was the main centre of the Polane People in the 8th century. A night view of the Old Town ▷▷
with its Gothic Cathedral. Five Polish Kings were crowned here.

Strzelno is one of Poland's oldest localities. The Romanesque rotunda of St. Procopius dates back to 1160.

Trzemeszno is a town in the Gniezno Lakeland area. ▷
Here the polychromed dome on the Late Baroque Church of the Assumption of the Blessed Virgin Mary.

Kórnik. Original castle from 1426, rebuilt in the English Gothic style in the 19th century.

Rogalin. The Rococo/Neo-Classical style Palace of the Raczyński Family. The Empire Study.

Rydzyna, an old Baroque town. A Baroque palace in an extensive landscaped park.

Gołuchów boasts a 16th century Renaissance castle ▷ remodelled in the style of the French Renaissance in the 19th century and set in picturesque English-style parkland.

Gostyń, with its Philippinian monastery complex,
Sanctuary to the Virgin Mary.

Klępsk. Renaissance wall-paintings
in the 16th century wooden church.

Poznań on the Warta, a capital of the historical Wielkopolska region. ▷
Ostrów Tumski with the Cathedral dating back to the 10th century.

Stud-farm at Golejewko with thoroughbred English horses.

◁ The Poznań Lakeland has a large number
of small, but highly picturesque, lakes.

Lake Wieleńskie, one of a number of lakes
dotting the Wielkopolska landscape.

Ląd. Gothic frescoes with the oldest surviving coats of arms of the Polish nobility in the town's Cistercian Monastery.

Syc ów. The gods of winter with a chest – one of four figures from the old castle offering allegories of the seasons of the year.

Książ boasts the imposing 16th century castle of the Hochbergs – the largest castle in Lower Silesia. It has often been remodelled, most notably in the Baroque style in the 18th century.

Karpacz. The 13th century Evangelical Wang Church brought from Norway in the 19th century.

THE MONGOLS CAME THIS FAR

Legnica was truly unfortunate. At its walls Duke Henry the Pious lost a decisive battle with the Tartar hordes in 1241. They came from the huge Mongol Empire united under Genghis Khan. When they invaded Europe, the Poles stood against them despite being divided into several dukedoms. All in vain. The prince and his best knights were killed. Nevertheless, weakened by their own losses, the Tartars decided not to proceed further to the west. Europe was saved.

Later Legnica, along with most of Silesia, was conquered by the Bohemians, then by the Habsburgs and the Prussian Hohenzollerns, Hitler's Nazis, and finally by that Genghis Khan of the 20th century – Joseph Stalin. He chose Legnica as his westernmost base and the main Soviet army quarters in Poland. Like the Mongols in the past, the stationed soldiers were prepared to attack the West.

The bad times have passed. Not a single Russian soldier is stationed in Poland any more. Legnica has been paid with good fortune, for it has became the centre of a dynamic copper industry. The present output amounts to 5 per cent of total world production and copper is accompanied by silver (7 per cent of world production). Silver, as we know, always comes with gold, but its output is a trade secret.

Silesia is one of the five main historic regions of Poland, along with Wielkopolska (Great Poland), Małopolska (Little Poland), Mazovia and Pomerania.

Silesia is divided into three parts. Lower Silesia borders with Germany on the River Nysa (Neisse); Upper Silesia has been the main industrial area in Poland for the last hundred years; Opole Silesia straddles the two.

The Sudetes are an attraction of Lower Silesia. These old mountains have been carved into fantastic shapes over time. There are plenty of rock cirques, winding ravines, scree slopes and strange rocky formations. The Sudetes consist of many ranges and massifs cut by deep valleys. The Karkonosze is the highest and steepest massif in the Sudetes, with the single barren peak of Śnieżka (1604 m) resembling a volcano, and otherwise a lunar landscape. A few holiday spots at the foothills of the Karkonosze, such as Karpacz and Szklarska Poręba, are frequented by skiers, though rather by beginners. An attraction in Karpacz is the early-13th century wooden church transferred here from

Wang in Norway and reconstructed
with great care.

The spacious low valley surrounded
by the Kaczawskie and Sowie Mountains, contains
the beautiful town of Jelenia Góra. It has some
Gothic and Baroque churches, a fine old market
square and some remains of medieval strongholds.

At the foothills of the Sudetes are a number
of small but often interesting towns. At Kowary,
an old factory continues to produce Smyrnean rugs,
while the uranium mine next to it has already
closed down. Chełmsko Śląskie has some charming
wooden weavers' houses from the beginning
of the 18th century while Krzeszów can boast
a 13th century Cistercian Abbey and one
of the most beautiful late-Baroque churches
in Poland. The imposing castle at Książ near
Wałbrzych, built in the 16th century over
much older foundations, is surrounded with
"hanging gardens" and a vast park
in the English style.

The next basin encompasses Kłodzko, a stronghold
on the route from Poland to the Czech lands from
the 10th century. Czech influence is clearly visible
in its architecture, for example in the Gothic bridge,
a replica of the Charles Bridge in Prague. Tourists
are fascinated by the massive fortress towering
above Kłodzko built by the King of Prussia,
Frederick II. Its dungeons are an object of studies
and a subject for thrillers.

From Kłodzko via a chain of spas: Polanica, Duszniki
Zdrój, where Frédéric Chopin gave concerts when
he was 16 and now piano music festivals are held,
and Kudowa we reach a peculiar part
of the Sudetes – the Stołowe (Table) Mountains.
From a distance they seem to be nothing special,
just some squat and flattened mountain ridge.
A surprise lies in wait as the visitor gets closer.
The upper parts are like a gigantic maze carved
by erosion, where you can roam for hours
on end seeing only a narrow strip of the sky above
and admiring all the strange rock shapes
resembling elephants, bears and eagle heads.

Many Lower Silesian towns are worthy of note.
Świdnica apparently used to be called "little
Cracow". Lubiąż has preserved the huge edifice
of the Cistercian Abbey, which looks like the famous
Escorial near Madrid and its cubature surpasses
that of the Wawel Castle in Cracow.

Wrocław, the capital of the region, is a peculiar city
– both for its great past and many historic relics,
including the Gothic Town Hall, and for its
fascinating present. In the last months
of the Second World War the city was turned
by the Nazis into anenormous citadel, die Festung

Breslau. Wrocław was almost as utterly destroyed
as Warsaw: 70 per cent of the houses lay in ruin.
Almost all German inhabitants fled to the West
or were deported after the war. Thousands of Poles
from various regions settled in the city, but initially
it was under the great influence of the intelligentsia
from Lviv (Lvov), a city lost by Poland to the Soviet
Union and now the major city of Western Ukraine.
Within a few years new Wrocław became a major
Polish city after Warsaw and Cracow. The local
university prospered and its school of mathematics
gained high international renown. Innovative
artistic trends developed. Jerzy Grotowski's
Laboratory Theatre was internationally recognized
as the revival of the theatre by drawing, among
others, from the art of ancient India. In the 1960s
Henryk Tomaszewski's pantomime theatre
won similar fame.

On Ostrów Tumski island in the old city centre,
life is focused around the imposing 13th century
Cathedral, surrounded by several other churches
and monasteries. Here reigns a serious mood born
of medieval mysticism.

It is amazing how quickly the new inhabitants
of Lower Silesia can integrate, no matter where
they come from. And they come from all parts
of the country, often from remote villages.
A lot of Poles have repatriated from the West:
France, Belgium, Westphalia, Britain, Yugoslavia,
Rumania or even Canada. Many Greeks
and Macedonians who settled in Wrocław
in the 1940s, the Ukrainians displaced from
the Bieszczady Mountains and the Lemeks from
the Beskid Niski became wholly Polonized.

In neighbouring Opole Silesia things were
a bit different. In some areas of this region
the autochthonous population of German descent
prevails (though before the Second World War
many of them regarded themselves as Poles
and were against uniting with Germany). Now they
have their own German institutions, schools
and unions. They delegate their own deputies
to the Sejm, at the same time staying loyal
to the Polish state.

Opole is a pleasant city with some old relics.
The most precious of them is the 14th century Piast
Tower. Once a year this peaceful town fills with
crowds of visitors from the whole country who
come to attend the popular Festival of Polish Song,
held in Opole for over 40 years.

The monument to Polish insurgents on St. Anne's
Mountain commemorates their fierce struggle
against the Germans after the First World War.
Today the monument is treated as a symbol
of Polish and German reconciliation and mutual
forgiveness of the harms inflicted.

In the east the Opole region merges with Upper Silesia, where in poet Julian Tuwim's words, "Coal and steel have their say".

In Upper Silesia the earth is black and ill with fatigue. Only men of business come here. Others would rather exclude the main Upper Silesian cities – Katowice, Chorzów, Zabrze, Bytom, Gliwice, as well as many smaller towns – from their itinerary, although there are quite a number of interesting sights in the area.

Only the southern edge of Upper Silesia – the mountains and their foothills – is free from fumes, noise and other kinds of pollution.

The Beskids offer good and very popular skiing facilities in the villages of Szczyrk, Wisła and Korbielów. At Koniaków and Istebna the enchanting folklore of the Beskid highlanders is still blooming. The nearby old Cieszyn, divided into the Polish and the Czech part by the River Olza, is Poland's main gate to the South.

One place name in the region fills everyone with terror. A symbol of the Holocaust – in German Auschwitz, in Polish Oświęcim. The site of the largest Nazi death camp, where millions of victims were gassed and burned. The majority of them were Jews. A visitor can only cry over their ashes.

The Karkonosze, a mountain range in the Sudetes with the highest peak, Śnieżka (1602 m), are especially beautiful in winter. ▷
The Głazy Krasnoludków (Dwarf Rocks) are picturesquely-situated sandstone erratics dropped by the retreating ice sheets south of today's Krzeszów. ▷▷

Walim, These mysterious underground corridors are what remain of German structures from World War II. Their purpose remains unknown to this day.

Wałbrzych. These mine towers of the former ▷
Wałbrzych Mine are above the Bolesław Chrobry face.

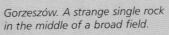

Gorzeszów. A strange single rock
in the middle of a broad field.

Świerzawa. Zoomorphic presentations of a Late
Romanesque painting in the apse of the Romanesque
Church of Sts. John the Baptist and Catherine.

Krzeszów. The Cistercian Abbey complex from the 17th century featuring ▷
the Late Baroque decoration within the Abbey Church of the Virgin Mary.

*Jawor. The Evangelical Church of the Holy Ghost or "Peace Church" is Early Baroque in style,
and shaped like a rectangle with four levels of seating. It can accommodate 6000 people.*

Książ – the Castle features nearly 400 rooms in various architectural styles.The Baroque Maximilian Room.

Strzegom. The monumental Gothic Cathedral of Saints Peter ▷
and Paul is built of granites and basalts from the nearby quarries.

Świdnica is an old market town still boasting an attractive architectural complex. Here the Old Town Market Square. ▷▷

Legnica. St. John's Church from the 18th century features this mausoleum to the Dukes of Legnica and Brzeg.

Kamieniec Ząbkowicki. The 19th century Neo-Gothic Castle was designed by Karl Friedrich Schinkel. It survived Second World War but has not been able to stand up to latter-day Polish vandals. ▷

178

◁ *Wrocław, the capital of Lower Silesia, is a historic city on the Oder which began life as a Slav settlement in the first millennium. The characteristic Gothic Town Hall, from the 14th-15th centuries.*

Trzebnica. The former Cistercian Convent Complex with its Church of Saints Bartholomew and Jadwiga and mansion-like Convent.

Oleśnica. The Castle of the Dukes of Oleśnica was erected in stages from the 13th century onwards. Here the arcaded Renaissance courtyard.

Małujowice is a locality along the trail of Brzeg polychromy. The St. James the Apostle Church interior is adorned by Mediaeval wall painting.

Brzeg, an old settlement on the Oder, has been destroyed ▷ many times. To be seen here is an 18th century polychromed wardrobe in a chamber of the Renaissance Town Hall.

Opole – a historic town on the Oder – is the capital of Opole Silesia.
This view of a fragment of the southern side of the market square
features 16th century tenement houses and the tower of the Church
of the Holy Trinity.

Moszna near Opole. Eclectic castle built ▷
at the end of the 19th century.

KOPALNIA WUJEK

Katowice. Wujek coal mine, a symbol of Polish resistance to martial law imposed in 1981.

◁ *The Milicz Ponds offer habitat for many rare species of waterbirds.*

The Upper Silesian Industrial District includes ▷▷
the Katowice Steelworks, which is actually just
beyond Silesia in the Zagłębie region.

Beskid Śląski is the furthest west of the Beskid ranges and is well-frequented by tourists. This view from Czantoria shows why.

Cieszyn. The 11th century Romanesque-style rotunda ▷ dedicated to St. Nicholas is situated on the tree-covered Castle Hill. It takes the form of a circle of diameter 6.4 m.

Members of the Śląsk folk ensemble in the traditional costume of the Beskidy Mountains.

Oświęcim, still better known to millions by its German name of Auschwitz, ▷▷ remains a symbol of the Holocaust. The site of the former Nazi concentration camp is today a museum recalling the full horror of what happened here.

Cracow. Known as the Cloth Hall, this former centre of trade is in the middle of the city's Main Market Square.

A little girl in Cracow dress.

The Cracow-Częstochowa Upland with its unusual rock forms.

THE HEART AND SOUL OF POLES

The region we are now approaching is most difficult to describe, for it can only be praised and that may raise the reader's doubts.

Before we come to the most beautiful Polish town, let us see a real wonder, a sight unique in the world: the Wieliczka salt mine. It was royal property, but in 1105 King Bolesław the Wry-mouthed conferred the privilege of collecting the income from the mine to the Benedictine Abbey at Tyniec. Later, the mine was leased to wealthy families, who amassed still greater riches from it. A similar mine was built in neighbouring Bochnia. Both are still exploited, though on a smaller scale. The old parts of the mine, extending to a depth of 315 metres, have been turned into a museum, which comprises a few hundred chambers and corridors, including the famous "crystal chambers" decorated with figures of saints carved in blocks of salt, altars, chandeliers and other ornaments.

From Wieliczka it is only a short distance to Cracow (Kraków). Tied by the neat ribbon of the River Vistula, the city boasts the most precious historic site and architectural complex in Poland: the castle and cathedral on Wawel Hill.

First comes the legend. Once upon a time, a terrible dragon dwelled in a cave in this hill. It would eat only the most beautiful virgins and in old times dragons had no reason to fear they would die of hunger. None of the knights of the wealthy Duke Krak was brave enough to fight with the dragon, though the promised splendid reward was marriage with the Duke's daughter. Only a simple shoemaker undertook the task. He tore the skin of a sheep, filled it with sulphur and tar and left it by the dragon's cave. The sheep must have appeared to the dragon more spicy than a virgin for the monster rushed to swallow it. Immediately, the beast's stomach set on fire. To put out the flames, it descended to the water and started to drink until it drank half of the river. Then it burst. The shoemaker got his reward – the princess, and Krak set up his residence on the hill rescued from dragon.

Some records indicate the Vislanes formed their little state a century earlier than the Polanes. According to The life of St. Methodius, a powerful pagan duke lived there. He refused to be baptized and "did harm to Christians", and eventually he was baptized by force in the foreign land. It may have been the Moravian state, ruling over the upper Vistula and Cracow for several decades at the turn of the 10th century. The land was then conquered by the Polanes. Gniezno and Poznań were the centres of the emerging Polish state. Around the mid-11th century Cracow grew in importance again and as the largest town in Poland and a major European trading centre, it started to play the role of a capital. When the Polish duchies were united at the beginning of the 14th century, Cracow grew into a big and rich town, worthy of the University founded by King Casimir the Great – the second one in Central Europe after the University of Prague, and older than any of the German universities.

Both the layout of that old Cracow and most of the houses within the old defensive walls have been preserved. On these old walls around the Old Town a green belt was laid out (called Planty i.e. Plantations), but certain fragments, such as the fine Barbican and Florian Gate have survived intact to this day.

The massive walls surrounding the Wawel have survived, too, together with the fine Renaissance Royal Castle and the Cathedral where Polish kings were crowned.

Wawel Castle is a museum with rich collections, such as one of the world's most valuable assemblies of wall carpets called arrasy (from Arras in France). There is a gallery of oriental art and the crown treasury, where the coronation sword of Polish kings, Szczerbiec, is kept. The Cathedral also dates back to the pre-Romanesque and Romanesque periods, but it is mainly Gothic in style. The nave is surrounded by eighteen Renaissance and Baroque chapels. The Sigismund Chapel, built by Bartolommeo Berecci, is considered to be one of the greatest Renaissance buildings in Europe. The last two Jagiellons, to whom Cracow owes a great deal, rest under its gilt roof: Sigismund the Old and Sigismund Augustus. The Gothic sarcophagus of Casimir the Great was made by Veit Stoss (in Polish Wit Stwosz), the famous sculptor of the end of the Gothic and the beginning of the Renaissance periods. Other priceless objects include King Władysław Jagiełło's favourite Byzantine-Ruthenian polychrome painting and the sarcophagus of St. Stanisław made by masters from Gdańsk in 1671. In the Cathedral treasury are housed splendid works of religious art, coronation insignia and St. Maurice's spear presented to King Bolesław the Brave by Emperor Otto III. The giant Sigismund Bell in the Cathedral tower, eight metres in circumference, sounds only on the most special state occasions.

The most precious of all is the whole Old Town of Cracow, which has preserved its medieval urban layout. Its most important sites are the Cloth Hall – a long 14th century market hall beautifully remodelled in the Renaissance period, the Gothic Town Hall Tower (the Town Hall building has not survived), the little Church of St. Adalbert from the end of the 11th century, and, above all, the imposing St. Mary's Church, built of brick and stone in the Gothic style with two differently finished towers. For hundreds of years a bugle-call has been sent out every hour from the higher tower and its sound always breaks in the middle. This is supposed to commemorate the 13th century trumpeter alarming the city whose throat was pierced by an arrow shot by a Tartar soldier. The high altar of the church was carved by Veit Stoss of Nuremberg who found a second homeland in Poland. This triptych, 11 m wide and 13 m high, is a masterpiece of late-Gothic sculpture.

Most houses surrounding the Cracow Market Square date from the 14th to 16th centuries. In spite of later alterations, their old architecture has been largely preserved.

Lovers of painting should not miss the Czartoryski Museum in Cracow. It boasts Leonardo da Vinci's "Lady with an Ermine", which in the opinion of many connoisseurs absolutely matches his "Mona Lisa", and Rembrandt's "Landscape with Good Samaritan".

Cracow has more than a dozen churches of great historic value and a few hundred such houses. The Jagiellonian Library collections comprise unique texts from the distant past.

A masterpiece of the Gothic style and the oldest part of the Jagiellonian University, the Collegium Maius, today serves as a museum of this ancient school. Among its exhibits, a 16th century globe on which America was marked for the first time in history and astronomical devices used by Nicolaus Copernicus are of particular interest.

Just a brief look at the environs of Cracow. At Bielany the domes of the Camaldolite Church and Monastery tower above the surrounding woods. On a rocky hill above the Vistula narrowing at Tyniec stand the age-old walls of the 11th century Benedictine Abbey.

The valley of the little River Prądnik, cutting a small mountain ridge near Cracow, is extremely attractive and quite unique. The steep canyon walls are ornamented with rocks in fantastic shapes, one of which is called the Hercules' Club. This is the area of the Ojców National Park, abounding in vegetation and historic monuments. The local caves provided shelter for palaeolithic men and mammoth hunters. Legend has it that in the 13th century they were a hiding-place of King Władysław the Short, the one who strove to unite Poland in times of feudal disintegration. At Pieskowa Skała, a magnificent 14th century Gothic-Renaissance castle stands proudly on a precipitous rock above the River Prądnik.

The Cracow-Częstochowa Upland, or Jura, a range of limestone hills destroyed by erosion and the movements of glaciers, initially rises at Ojców. The strangely-shaped island mountains known in Polish as ostańce are quite an attraction, and many of them contain the ruins of medieval castles; Tenczyn, Rabsztyn, Smoleń Bobolice, Mirów, Ogrodzieniec (at 504 m the highest of all), Morsko and Olsztyn are but some examples.

In the west, the Jura neighbours with a Polish curiosity, which unfortunately is gradually disappearing: the Błędowska Desert. It possesses all the characteristics of a desert except camels. Mirages have been recorded. But the local dunes have been used for industrial purposes and housing spreads towards the desert outskirts.

In the north, the Jura gets lower until it merges with the level upland and disappears amid towns and industrial plants. At its other end lies the town of Częstochowa with its treasure, Jasna Góra (Bright Mountain). Known as the "Polish Lourdes", it is a popular sanctuary and goal of countless pilgrimages by the faithful. The darkened, beautiful Gothic chapel of the huge early-14th century Pauline Monastery on the mountain top contains the famous icon of the Black Madonna. This magnificent image of the Holy Virgin Mary, set on an inlaid ebony altar, has for ages drawn millions of pilgrims seeking their conciliation in the thoughtful eyes of the Madonna. When partitioned Poland suffered the slavery imposed on it by its three neighbouring powers, this image of the Virgin Mary, the patroness and Queen of the Poles, symbolically enthroned by King John Casimir in gratitude for saving the country from the Swedish "Deluge", united all Poles and reminded them of their duties toward the enslaved but still alive Fatherland.

Cracow. Wawel, on a limestone hill overlooking the Vistula comprises ▷
the Gothic-Renaissance Royal Castle, Gothic Cathedral and defensive walls.

Cracow's Royal Cathedral is the most important place of worship to be associated with the history of the whole nation. Coronations, royal weddings and funerals took place here.

Cracow's Wawel Hill with the Castle Courtyard and its Renaissance column-arcaded cloisters.

Cracow. The Monument to Tadeusz Kościuszko, leader of the victorious Polish ▷ forces in the Battle of Racławice fought against the Russians in 1794.

Cracow. The Main Market Square
(Rynek Główny) with the Cloth Hall
and Gothic-style Church of the Virgin Mary.

Cracow. This Lajkonik from the Premonstratensian
(Norbertine) Convent in Zwierzyniec appears
on the Main Market Square each year in time
for the celebration of Corpus Christi.

Cracow – St. Mary's Church. ▷
Detail of the altar carved by Veit Stoss in lime wood in 1477-89.

Cracow. The Main Market Square is one of the largest Mediaeval squares in Europe. ▷▷
The view features the Cloth Hall, as well as the Churches of St. Mary and St. Adalbert.

Cracow. Floriańska Street links the Florian Gate with the Main Market Square and is a section of the Royal Route.

Cracow. The procession of the Kurkowy Brotherhood makes its way towards the Church on the Rock.

Cracow. The 11th century Romanesque-style Church of St. Andrew is in Grodzka Street.

Cracow. Serving as a centrepiece on St' Mary's ▷ Square is a well with figure of a schoolby which is a copy of a sculpted figure on the altar in the Church.

Niepołomice features a Renaissance Castle rebuilt from a Gothic predecessor in the 16th century with a view to its serving as a hunting residence for the King. The square courtyard with arcaded cloistered is modelled on that at the Wawel Castle.

◁ *Nowy Wiśnicz. The Baroque-style fortyfied residence of the Lubomirski Family. The Castle's characteristic silhouette with its corner towers.*

Kalwaria Zebrzydowska. The Baroque Basilica
of the Angelic Mother of God and Bernardine Monastery.

Ojców in the Prądnik Valley, a holiday and health resort since the 19th ▷
century, the centre of Ojców National Park. Castle Road.

Ojców. The old trees hark back to the former Zdrojowy Park. ▷▷

Ogrodzieniec. Characteristic rocks in the Cracow-Częstochowa Upland.

Potok Złoty. The characteristic limestone rock known as the Twardowski Gate.

Mirów. A 14th century castle in ruins.

Smoleń. Ruins of the Gothic castle from the 14th century are ▷
located picturesquely among the limestone rocks.

Potok Złoty, with its Palace Park and pond. ▷▷

Częstochowa. The miraculous likeness of the Black Madonna of Jasna Góra.

◁ *Częstochowa and Jasna Góra, with monks processing to the Chapel of St. Paul the First Hermit, patron of the Pauline Order.*

Olsztyn near Częstochowa. Scenic ruins of the 14th century ▷▷ *castle set in the landscape of the Cracow-Częstochowa Upland.*

THE EUROPEAN FLINT TOOL CENTRE

White storks on the nest are a feature of the Polish landscape to be enjoyed across the country.

Krzemionki, the biggest neolithic flint mine in Europe, a historic monument. The reconstruction of a settlement.

Four thousand years ago the chipped flint industry was a major branch of production. Flint is a hard stone. Flint tools were good for loosening soil and killing game – and of course enemies. The area of Krzemionki near Ostrowiec Świętokrzyski is recognized as the greatest European flint basin of the neolithic period. The raw material was dug deep in the ground and it was chipped into tools and arms on the spot.

Local axes were an export product as important as tanks today. They have been excavated from the Ukraine to the River Elbe in Germany. They are easily recognizable, for they are all marked with stripes. A large mining field of our neolithic forefathers has been preserved at Krzemionki. It had as many as 3,000 shafts, some of which were 10 to 12 metres in diameter and about the same depth. The shafts were connected by underground tunnels, which were shored up and ventilated through special holes. The ancient mine is a unique archaeological reserve and a precious prehistoric site.

Industrial activity was continued in Roman times. In the 1st and 2nd centuries A.D. the area specialized in metallurgy. Metal tools, nails, swords and spearheads were smelted, also for export.

Those industrial traditions were revived in the Kielce region a few centuries ago. Copper, silver, lead and iron ores from the Świętokrzyskie (Holy Cross) Mountains began to be extracted and processed on a greater scale. The Old Polish Industrial Centre developed around the ancient, worn-out mountains.

Today the mountains are still overgrown with the famous fir forest, turned into a national park, though industrial pollution mainly from the local cement mills and lime kilns has caused a serious decline of forest. The remains of old industrial constructions from the 18th and 19th century, e.g. the metallurgical furnaces at Samsonów and the dam at Nietulisko, are protected as historic monuments. Another tourist attraction, the biggest (13.4 m in trunk diameter) and oldest oak tree in Poland, called Bartek, must remember the times of Mieszko I.

The highest points of the Świętokrzyskie Mountains are Łysica (612 m), also called St. Catherine, and Łysa Góra, or Holy Cross (595 m), covered with boulder fields. In the 8th and 9th centuries a major centre of pagan cult in Poland existed on Łysa Góra. Some fragments of its walls have survived.

Tokarnia. The inside of a hut at the outdoor ethnographic museum.

To bring an end to paganism, King Bolesław the Wry-mouthed founded the Benedictine Abbey on Łysa Góra at the onset of the 12th century. In the 19th century it was turned into an infamous prison. Today the monastic complex is administered by some tourist organizations. Next to it a 138-metre television broadcasting tower has been raised, offering a wide view of the surroundings. Some traces of pagan cults have survived in folk legends, in which Łysa Góra is described as a meeting place of witches, flying up there on broomsticks from all over the country.

Kielce, the capital of the region, existed as early as the 11th century as a trading settlement. Initially it was owned by the archbishops of Cracow, then – as a "liberated town" – it grew into the main centre of the Old Polish Industrial Basin (the name coined by contemporary historians). Before Poland was finally partitioned, Kielce was incorporated into the royal estate in 1789. Unlike its environs, the city itself has not much to offer to tourists. Only the 17th century Bishops' Palace with early-Baroque interiors and a beautiful Baroque arcaded house in the Market Square with a museum rich in ethnographic collections remind us of Kielce's past glory.

On great occasions Kielce folklore can be witnessed spontaneously in some villages. As the regional costumes are ornate and expensive, they are passed from mothers to daughters and from fathers to sons. When put on, they are quite a show.

The picturesque Baroque Benedictine Monastery on Karczówka hill near Kielce stands out from the city. In the nearby Chęciny, massive ruins of a fortified castle built by King Casimir the Great have survived on a hilltop. The historic town at its foot has narrow streets lined with several hundred year-old burghers' houses and two monasteries: of the Franciscans and the Poor Clares. Fragments of streets and squares laid with fine marble from the local quarries have been preserved.

Radom is Kielce's rival town, almost equally old but completely industrialized. A lot of historic relics have survived, some of them dating back to the 14th century. However, Radom is known best for its tradition of revolutionary struggle, the workers' rebellion against the communist regime in 1976 in particular. It prompted the activity of the Committee to Defend the Workers (KOR), which already operated half-openly. Its members later became the chief leaders and consultants of Solidarity.

History dwells in the walls of castles, churches and in cemeteries of many little towns and villages of the Kielce region. At Szydłowiec, where sandstone was mined for building material as early as the Middle Ages, the 15th century castle of the Szydłowiecki family has been preserved. It was later rebuilt by the Radziwiłłs, the famous Lithuanian-Polish aristocratic family related to some ruling dynasties in the West, into one of their countless residences. The Town Hall has retained its pure early-Renaissance form and beautifully carved 18th century tombstones can be seen at the historic Jewish cemetery.

At the village of Szydłów a complex of historic buildings has survived. It comprises the 14th century castle and Parish Church with a fragment of defence walls and the fine Cracow Gate, as well as a synagogue from later times.

The Cistercian Abbey at Wąchock is older still. Founded in 1179, it is a good example of the transition period between the Romanesque and the Gothic styles in architecture. The Cistercian Order, a model of medieval piety and good husbandry, evidently favoured that style. The Collegiate Church at Opatów dating from the same period was extended and beautifully decorated.

The Świętokrzyski (or Kielce) region is famous for its karst caves shrouded in legends. The most beautiful and frequented Raj (Paradise) Cave near Chęciny is adorned with stalactites and stalagmites of fantastic shapes. Thus, the region offers everything a tourist looks for: traces of ancient history, natural wonders, masterpieces of architecture and rich folklore, not to mention devils and witches.

Krzcięcice near Jędrzejów. The springtime thaw. ▷▷

Szydłowiec has been known since the Middle Ages for its is Szydłowiecki sandstones, used in the facing of buildings to this day. Looking down the street we see the Late Gothic Church of St. Sigismund.

Wąchock, a flint tool centre in the Stone Age.
The Cistercian Abbey.

Kielce is a town situated at the edge of the Świętokrzyskie Mountains with a history ▷
extending back to the 11th century. The perfectly preserved Palace of the Bishops of Cracow
is representative of a style transitional between those of the Renaissance and the Baroque period.

Jaskinia Raj (the "Paradise Cave") with its outstanding stalactites, stalagmites and rock formations. Traces of the presence of Neanderthal Man have been found here.

Chęciny. Picturesque ruins of a 15th century castle. ▷

Spring meadows in the Kielce region. ▷▷

The Świętokrzyskie Mountains are mostly gentle and forest-covered.

◁ *Tokarnia. Ethnographic Park of the Museum of the Kielce Countryside, a peasant farm.*

The Chęciny area astounds the visitor each year with its amazing numbers of flowering poppies.

Tokarnia. The interior of a hut equipped in the original way is to be seen in the Outdoor Museum of the Kielce Countryside.

The Vistula near Dęblin meanders widely, creating bays and islands.

WHERE THE VISTULA IS MOST BEAUTIFUL

Very few Polish towns have been praised so much by Polish writers as Sandomierz on the Vistula where that river is joined by the San.

The town is beautiful. Its priceless oldest historic building is the former Dominican Church of St. James, built of brick in 1226. Art lovers will admire the Gothic Cathedral with unique and perfectly retained 15th century frescoes in the Byzantine-Old Russian style. They recall the time when Sandomierz was a major centre of trade at the crossing of roads to Ruthenia and Hungary. The Sandomierz townsfolk prospered and built fine houses. One of those houses belonged to the famous 15th century Polish chronicler Jan Długosz. The town flourished in the Renaissance period, when the Town Hall with a fine parapet wall was built, as well as the Market Square houses. In Baroque times the Benedictine Monastery, St. Paul's Church and a synagogue were added. Among curious objects are some bone chess pieces from the 11th century excavated by archaeologists. Among curious events, in 1843 a flood swept away several dozens ancient coffins from the cathedral vaults waiting outside for cremation and floated them down the river scaring local peasants to death. Among the legends, there is one saying that a mad bull once engraved the inscription Salve Regina with its horn on an ancient mound to make people more pious.

The old architecture of Sandomierz makes a wonderful sight on the high Vistula escarpment, with the river meandering at the foot of the town between the edges of the Kielce-Sandomierz and Lublin uplands. Pressed by its several swift Carpathian tributaries, the Vistula shifts its bed all the time. Watched from above, the numerous old river beds look like a whirling mass of snakes.

The village of Wrzawa at the marshy confluence of the Vistula and the San has a very bad reputation among the locals from the Sandomierz Forest. They imagine the area to be the gate to hell. The surrounding bogs, quagmires and wicker are crowded with kelpies, lamias, nymphs and other water spirits, while on drier land common devils roam. However, they are pretty hard to meet these days. Maybe they have been frightened off by TV and cars, or got intoxicated by sulphurous exhausts.

For, on the other bank of the Vistula almost exactly opposite Sandomierz, lies Tarnobrzeg, the centre of the sulphur industry

Gołąb. The Early Baroque Loretańska Chapel from 1640, with its ceramic reliefs of the prophets.

Sandomierz. Interior of the Cathedral of the Blessed Virgin Mary.

existing for 40 years and bringing high profits to Poland from its exports.

The huge fortified Krzyżtopór castle at Ujazd was erected in the 17th century on a pentagonal plan by Italian architect Lorenzo Senes. Built for the Ossoliński family, it was to symbolize their power and glory, and most of all their solidity. The number of castle towers equals that of the seasons of the year; there are as many halls as months, as many chambers as weeks and as many windows as days in the year. The designer's (or his employers') fantasy went so far as to replace the ceiling of one chamber in the biggest bastion with an aquarium full of exotic fish. It is a great pity that this excellent example of Mannerism was reduced to ruin only a decade after its building, i.e. in 1655 during the Swedish "Deluge". Another reminder of the Ossoliński family's generosity is the church at Klimontów, also abounding in strange and quite impractical solutions.

And so the picturesque River Vistula, enveloped in legends reaches the town of Kazimierz Dolny – even more beautiful than Sandomierz, if this is at all possible. It is here that painters have been coming by the thousands for a century now to contemplate and paint nature. Kazimierz is the town they love most, next only to Cracow. The charming Renaissance and Baroque town spreading over several hills and deep ravines has become Poland's, and especially Warsaw's, open-air salon. The well-maintained houses of rich burghers: the Przybyła (late-Renaissance), the Gdańsk (Baroque) and the Celej (Mannerist) houses have fine gables and richly ornamented façades. When sightseeing in Poland you can skip a lot of towns, but certainly not Kazimierz. Nearby on the right bank of the Vistula we find another attraction – Puławy. At the end of the 18th and the beginning of the 19th centuries this residence of the powerful Czartoryski family functioned as an extension of the capital. It was an important political, cultural and philosophical centre competing with Warsaw. While the modern trend of the Enlightenment reigned at the court of Stanisław Augustus Poniatowski, at Puławy they were in for sentimentalism. After the king's abdication the Czartoryski family were treated with such respect as if they were a substitute dynasty for the time of enslavement. They remodelled the former Baroque Lubomirski Palace into a neoclassical residence, surrounded by an unusually beautiful park with a romantic Temple of Sibyl encircled with Doric columns.

In the neighbouring spa town of Nałęczów, with mineral water rich in iron, two great writers, Bolesław Prus and Stefan Żeromski, liked to stay and strengthen their hearts. Żeromski, a dissident struggling against the Tsar, set up a clandestine political centre at Nałęczów camouflaged as some educational institutions and cooperatives. A majority of state leaders in the soon-to-be-independent Poland were instructed there. At the opposite, south-eastern end of the Lublin region lies Zamość, which fully deserves its qualification as "a pearl of the Renaissance". Quite untypically, the town was designed and built on virgin land by the rich family of Jan Zamoyski, Chancellor and Grand Hetman of the Crown. He was the chief adviser to King Stephen Bathory, a Hungarian from Transylvania with a poor command of the language of the country he ruled. The king owed many of his successes to Jan Zamoyski, whose greatest merit was Zamość, designed and built by the Italian Bernardo Morando.

Having travelled around the whole region, let us now visit its main city. Lublin is very old; the first settlement dates to the 8th or 9th century. From the 12th century it served as a base for eastward Polish expansion into the Ukraine. In return, it was often invaded by Lithuanians, Tartars and Ruthenians. The union of the Polish Kingdom and the Grand Duchy of Lithuania was signed in Lublin in 1569.

Of Lublin's numerous historic places, the Royal Castle is the most valuable. Its beginning dates back to the 14th century, but only the tower and Gothic Trinity Chapel have survived from that time. The Chapel contains a real treasure: the excellent Ruthenian-Byzantine murals founded by King Władysław Jagiełło around 1385. The city has a vast collection of churches in every style met in the Polish lands – from Gothic to neoclassical.

At the end of 1944 and the beginning of 1945 Lublin was a temporary capital of Poland, where the Soviet-imposed Polish Committee of National Liberation resided. This sad fact is better forgotten.

Janowiec. The attractive ruins of Mikołaj Firlej's 16th century castle by the Vistula.

Piaseczno. This strange landscape arose in a place where sulphur was once mined. ▷

Tarnobrzeg in the Sandomierz Valley, is a sulphur industry centre. The Tarnowski Palace.

Sandomierz is a beautiful example of architectural and town planning. This photograph shows the Market Square with its Renaissance Town Hall.

The Kazimierz Dolny area – a deep canyon cut through ▷ the loess soil is mysterious enough to tempt the walker.

Ujazd. Ruins of the Mannerist Krzyżtopór Castle.

Nałęczów is a famous spa with potable mineral waters.

Puławy on the Vistula. Baroque palace remodelled in the neoclassical style, surrounded by an old park.

◁ *Kazimierz Dolny was founded in the 12th century by King Casimir II the Just, and developed during the reign of his namesake Casimir the Great. Today it is a town full of artists.*

Kazimierz Dolny enjoys a picturesque location by the Vistula, as well as a Renaissance architectural layout. Here the view from Krzyżowa Góra. ▷▷

*Okrzeja. Polychromy in the Baroque/Neo-Classical church portrays scenes
from Henryk Sienkiewicz's fable novel Potop ("The Deluge"),
and specifically the defence of Jasna Góra.*

*Zamość. The Mannerist-Baroque style Town Hall from the 17th century ▷
features a 52-metre tower and monumental 18th century steps.*

*Zamość is a city with a unique Renaissance architectural layout and town plan. 17th century
arcaded tenement houses on the Old Market Square recall the Renaissance architecture of Italy.*

*Lublin. From the 12th century onwards this was a fortified town devastated
at regular intervals by invaders from the east. This facade is of the 14th century
castle rebuilt in the neo-Gothic style at the beginning of the19th century.*

*Kozłówka. The Neo-Baroque style palace-park ▷
complex of the Zamoyski Family; the Palace façade
from the courtyard.*

Lublin. The Gothic Chapel of the Holy Trinity dates from the mid 14th century, and is supported by a single column.
The interiors are decorated by unique Byzantine-Russian frescoes funded by King Władysław Jagiełło.

THE VESTIBULE TO THE EAST

Lake Solińskie, an artificial reservoir good for water sports and recreation.

In the south-eastern corner of Poland on the River San a beautiful town extends over seven hills like Rome. Przemyśl is a specific town, for it lies on the border of two civilizations: Roman and Byzantine. Since the dawn of its history, i.e. the 10th century, Przemyśl has been an object of Polish-Ruthenian conflicts. They still echo today as the disputes over some places of worship, to which both the Roman Catholic majority and the Greek Catholic minority claim their rights. The latter, mostly Ukrainians, recognize papal supremacy but have remained faithful to their eastern rite. Luckily, these epic quarrels do not spoil the steadily improving relations between Poland and its big neighbour, Ukraine.

A magnificent view of the town extends from Castle Hill, where some fragments of the Renaissance castle built over much older, probably pre-Romanesque foundations have been preserved. Although the town is dominated by the Baroque style, it has a somewhat "Eastern" atmosphere. The local museum boasts a splendid collection of icons, closely connected with the eastern rite. Przemyśl will be interesting for those who study the mingling of cultures and for military art lovers. The town, which used to be one of the strongest forts of modern Europe, fiercely fought over during the First World War, is still encircled by imposing 19th century Austrian fortifications.

Przemyśl is an ages-old bone of territorial contention between Poland and Russia. Here a fountain with the city's bear symbol.

The environs are quite interesting. The village of Haczów in the Dynów Foothills is inhabited by Swedes, the descendants of Swedish soldiers taken prisoner in the 17th century. Although completely Polonized, they are still aware of their origins. Some areas are inhabited by Boyeks and Lemeks, a people close to Ukrainians. They cherish their traditions and (less and less often) their dialect.

The region abounds in palatial ensembles. The Krasicki Palace at Krasiczyn, built by the Italian Appiani (the Poles in the past liked to employ Italian architects!), is one of the most precious examples of the late Renaissance with some ornamental Mannerist details. The stately fortified early-Baroque castle of the Potocki, and earlier Lubomirski, families, at Łańcut, houses a museum of carriages. Sieniawa has the residence of the Sieniawski, later Czartoryski, families. Jarosław, which dates back to the times of King Bolesław Chrobry, offers quite an attraction: the vast, multilevel cellars and dungeons under the Old Town are open to visitors. The huge organ in the Bernardine Church at Leżajsk, set in the extremely opulent Baroque and Rococo interior, is said to match or even surpass that in Oliwa Cathedral. Sanok lacks great historic buildings, but its museum in the former Royal Castle owns

Krasiczyn. The Renaissance-Mannerist Krasicki Palace.

the largest icon collection in Poland, the oldest of which come from the 14th century. The arcaded burghers' houses at Krosno date back to the 16th century and the tower of the late-Gothic Parish Church contains the second biggest bell in Poland next to the Zygmunt in Cracow – the Urban bell weighing 5 tons.

The countryside is rather poor. Most of the 19th century Polish emigrants to the dreamland of America came from this region. The area underwent a short period of prosperity when oil was discovered here. The invention of the refining process and the construction of the first kerosene lamp by Polish engineer Ignacy Łukasiewicz at the village of Bóbrka instigated the worldwide career of the oil industry. And what progress – no more candles! Unfortunately, the Carpathian oil resources turned out to be small and they were used up quickly. Although some oil rigs still exist, they are monuments of technology rather than having any significant economic meaning. Of greater importance are the mineral springs at Rymanów and Iwonicz, where the saline waters with high iodine and bromine content have strong medicinal properties.

More spas – Żegiestów, known for its waters with high iron content, Piwniczna and picturesque Rytro – lie westwards in the vicinity of Nowy Sącz, in the past a market town on the route to Hungary, now an important centre of mountain tourism. The most famous of Polish health resorts (apart from Ciechocinek) is Krynica. Its mild climate and highly curative waters attract growing numbers of visitors. Some of them come for health, some for entertainment. In the period between the two world wars the world-famous Polish tenor Jan Kiepura used to come and stay in Krynica.

In the most distant tip of Poland, squeezed between Ukraine and Slovakia, the Bieszczady Mountains stretch wild and beautiful, forming the Bieszczady National Park. The least populated region of Poland, least interfered with by man's economic activity, has very few roads. The hills covered by deciduous and mixed forests and by vast meadows called połoniny, where grass is waist-high, tempt bold hikers, as do clean streams running through tunnels of greenery and the artificial Lake Solińskie, perfectly fitting into the landscape. The land is ideal for tourists who look for pristine nature rather than luxury. They will find large areas of forest, meadows and bushes around the massifs of Tarnica, Halicz and Wielka Rawka, where it is easier to spot a bear's footprint than a man's. Some dozen bears live in the area and many more wolves. Quick-moving lynx and wild cat occur, to say nothing of deer and boar. Watch the ground carefully not to tread on a viper. Living in trees not far away are a small number of large non-venomous Aesculapian snakes,

Kalwaria Pacławska, an 18th century Franciscan monastic complex. Church interiors.

a species completely extinct in Poland outside the Bieszczady region.

Whoever likes horror stories should pay a visit to the little town of Biecz, once called "little Cracow". Apart from a number of Gothic and Renaissance historic monuments and fragments of medieval fortifications, the somewhat grim attraction of the town's history was the school of public executioners, which trained masters in the craft, then hired for a fat fee by other towns. No one else knew so well how to inflict long and cruel tortures upon wrongdoers. Today some Biecz dwellers want to deny the "black story" of their town, while others are proud of it, for in their view every field of activity demands the attaining of perfection.

Rzeszów, the capital of the region, has but a few historic relics. Worth seeing are the 19th century pseudo-Gothic Town Hall and the monastery complexes of the Bernardine and Piarist monks, including the Regional Museum.

Leżajsk on the outskirts of Sandomierz Forest. Magnificent 17th century organ in the Bernardine Church.

Sieniawa. The 17th century ▷ Baroque palace in a large park.

*Nozdrzec near Dynów is a village
steeped in the landscape
of the Dynów Foothills.*

*Łańcut. Castle in the French
neo-Baroque style.*

*Rzeszów on the River Wisłok, first settled
n the neolithic period. The Market square with
the Town Hall remodelled in the 19th century.*

*Dachnów near Lubaczów has an old ▷
18th century Orthodox church built of wood in the shape of a Latin cross.*

◁ *Kolbuszowa. Ethnographic Park with the museum of regional building methods.*

Sanok. The Museum of Folk Architecture.

Lesko. The Jewish cemetery with its interesting tombstones.

The River San meanders through ▷▷ the Bieszczady Mountains.

Zalipie. The "Painted Village", where local tradition dictates that houses, other buildings and household equipment should all be painted.

The Carpathian Foothill region ▷ of Podkarpacie.

Stary Sącz is a small town which retains its street plan from the Middle Ages. The Market Square is cobbled with what are known as "cat's heads"

Stary Sącz lies in the fork of the Dunajec ▷▷ and Poprad Rivers.

Crocuses proliferate in the spring meadows of the Chochołowska Valley.

In the Podhale region, the young wear their traditional Highland dress with pride.

The landscape of the Western Tatras looking from the Strążyska Valley towards Giewont.

FOR DESSERT – THE TATRAS

It is hard to believe that people in the past hated the mountains. In the Middle Ages they were considered unworthy of any attention, awful and dangerous, just standing in the way. In the early Renaissance, mountains were in favour for a short while, admired by Dante and Petrarch.
But the fascination was short-lasting. In the 16th century Montaigne called mountains (and seas) the most boring things in the world. Outstanding naturalist Buffon thought that "nature in its primeval state is dead and repulsive". Voltaire treated the Alps as an obstacle that divided nations.

The world has made progress, for most people today love mountains and regard them as the most wonderful phenomenon.

The Poles, especially those who have never seen any other mountain ranges, claim that the Tatras are the most beautiful of all mountains. Foreign visitors are also ready to admit that – the Alps being twice and the Himalayas four times as high – the Tatra scenery is really of comparable beauty.

But before we venture to the very brink of Poland, the Tatra summits, it is well worth making a detour to the east in order to visit the Pieniny Mountains. Only half as high as the Tatras, the miniature Pieniny are a real gem. At their foot runs the swift Dunajec, which offers a thrilling experience: a trip by raft over the rapids and cascades of its gorge.

The highest Pieniny massif, Trzy Korony (the Three Crowns) is only 982 metres high, but it is extremely diversified in form, with barren walls, sheer drops of two hundred metres, jagged rocks and ravines. The most popular is the Homole ravine in the Little Pieniny, higher then the main ridge. The fauna and flora are unique, abounding in rare species untypical for other Polish mountains, with many endemic ones not occurring anywhere outside the Pieniny. They are protected by the national park, now threatened by the dammed water of the Dunajec, the project carried out despite strong protests and demonstrations by the ecologists and young supporters of the green movement.

On fine days, the majestic range of the Tatra Mountains, piercing the clouds with its sharp peaks, is visible from many distant localities of the Cracow region. The most splendid view of the Tatras is from the deep basin of Podhale, the region of Highlanders, a proud people gifted with exuberant imagination and using their own dialect. They reveal enormous artistic talents. Their music and dance, architecture, wood-carving and sculpture, their legends and funny folk tales are a jewel in Polish folklore. In the villages at the foot of the Tatras the highland traditions sparkle with life. Here the colourful and ornate Highlanders' costumes are worn not only on special occasions. The rich folk culture of the Podhale region bears many traces of influence from the neighbouring pastoral peoples, such as the Rumanian Valachians, Moldavians, Slovaks and Hungarians, as well as those of settlers from historic Ruthenia and Germany, and numerous Gypsies.

The Tatras are the highest and the most diversified range of the long Carpathian chain – young mountains almost untouched by erosion. The highest summits of the Tatras are Gerlachovka (2655 m) and Lomnicky (2632), both in Slovakia. Most of the Tatras lie outside Poland. Some peaks lie on the Polish-Slovak border, like Rysy, the north-western top of which is the highest peak in Poland, and Kasprowy Wierch most important for skiers as the only peak accessible by cable car and two chair-lifts. In order to protect the tranquil environment for alpine animal species, such as chamois, marmot and bears, the Tatra National Park management categorically refuses permission to install any other skiing or tourist facilities.

Strict rules of environmental protection apply to the whole Tatras. Hopefully, they will not be moderated in spite of the skiers' unceasing protests. It is to these regulations that we owe fresh spring meadows carpeted with violet crocuses, crystalline water in lively mountain streams, and still a great deal of wild and inaccessible Tatra backwoods, where only the most experienced hikers can sometimes get. The magnificent Tatra lakes have also maintained their natural state and pure water. Lake Morskie Oko (34.5 ha) at the foot of the sheer crags of Mięguszowieckie Turnie enchants everyone.

Giewont, towering over Zakopane, is a symbol of the town. An easy tourist trail ascends at the back of the mountain, but the difficult and dangerous north wall presents a constant challenge to amateur mountain climbers. Dozens of them have lost their lives. Giewont is also a cult place, connected with the legend about the Sleeping Knights, similar to folk tales of many European countries. The knights from Giewont are a great puzzle, for the legend has about a dozen versions, differing from one another on such issues as when they fell asleep and why, who put them to sleep and what for and when they are going to wake up. If we accept the prevailing view that when they wake up, they will free Poland from foreign rule, they should surely be by now awake.

The narrow Tatra valleys squeezed deep in the mountains are no less popular than the peaks. Year by year thousands of vacationers come to walk there and breathe some invigorating mountain air. Most of these valley promenades are situated

The Western Tatras. The Kościeliska Valley in its winter cloak.

in the Western Tatras, slightly lower and gentler than the High Tatras.

In the past, the Podhale region was full of highwaymen, not legendary at all. The highlanders' favourite hero, named Janosik, lived and robbed on the southern, Slovakian side of the Tatras. He has been immortalized in countless songs, plays, novels, paintings and music pieces. Like Robin Hood, he robbed the rich and helped the poor. For his moral conduct he was caught and tried and sent to the gallows in 1713.

The lowlanders continue to cherish the myth of an old Zakopane, a wooden village at the mountain foot which at the beginning of the 20th century was so darling to the greatest Polish musicians, painters, writers, philosophers and politicians. Forty, maybe thirty years ago it still looked like that. Today it is a big town – not too beautiful, not very coherent and very crowded. No matter what, a trip to Zakopane is a must at least once a year. Not even the youngest generation would give up this tradition.

The Dunajec Gorge, a beautiful river canyon cutting
through the Pieniny Mountains. On a raft trip.

Frydman, a village by the Czorsztyn reservoir
with beautiful wooden houses.

Trybsz has a wooden church with interesting ▷
Baroque polychromy from 1674.

Czarna Góra is in the Polish part of the Spisz Elevation. On the Korkosz Farm the "Big Room" features ethnographic exhibits.

Olcza, a village of Highlanders, is today just a suburb of Zakopane, but still one that nestles beautifully in the surrounding hills.

Nowe Bystre is a Podhale village on the northern ▷ side of the Gubałówka Ridge.

*Bukowina Tatrzańska, a big Highlanders'
village. Interior of an old church.*

◁ *Nowe Bystre. A storm is not far away...*

Harenda is a peripheral Highland settlement of Zakopane. ▷▷
It has very largely retained its rural, agricultural character.

Zakopane. Heritage in the form of the old home
of the Gąsienica and Bednarz families
in Kościeliska Street.

Zakopane, the most popular holiday resort
in Poland since the 19th century Krupówki
is the main street of the town.

Zakopane. Kościeliska Street
– an old mountain homestead.

Zakopane. The Chapel at Jaszczurówka, built in the Zakopane ▷
style conceived by Stanisław Witkiewicz.
Ząb near Zakopane. A Colourful Corpus Christi procession. ▷▷

Zakopane. Leaders of a Highlanders'
wedding cavalcade invite guests.

◁ *Podhale. A view of the Tatras from the slopes of Gubałówka.*

Grazing sheep at Lipki near Zakopane.

◁ *The Miętusia Valley is a branch of the Kościeliska Valley cutting into the Czerwone Wierchy massif.*

The High Tatras and Roztoka Valley. An interesting and picturesque tourist trail runs along the valley floor.

The Tatras are the loftiest and most diverse massif in the Western Carpathians. Here we see Mnich ("The Monk") above the mountain tarn known as Morskie Oko ("The Sea's Eye").

In the High Tatras, the Mickiewicz Falls along the Roztoka Stream can be viewed just by the road leading to Morskie Oko. ▷
Polana Zahradziska in the Kościeliska Valley of the Western Tatras. ▷▷

Poland

Photography:
CHRISTIAN PARMA

Text:
WOJCIECH GIEŁŻYŃSKI

Layout,
captions to photographs,
editor:
BOGNA PARMA

Translation:
ELŻBIETA KOWALEWSKA
PETER MARTYN
JAMES RICHARDS

DTP:
Studio PARMA

Publisher:
Wydawnictwo PARMA PRESS Sp. z o.o.
05 270 Marki, al. Piłsudskiego 189 b
+48 22/ 781 16 48, 781 16 49, 781 12 31
e-mail: wydawnictwo@parmapress.com.pl
http://www.parmapress.com.pl

ISBN 83-7419-000-0

© Copyright by Wydawnictwo PARMA® PRESS Sp. z o.o.

Marki 2007

Illustration on the cover:
Niedzica features a partially-ruined for which gained itself
a fine location when a reservoir filled behind the Czorsztyn dam.